MEETING *Islam*

A Guide for Christians

George Dardess

PARACLETE PRESS
BREWSTER, MASSACHUSETTS

Library of Congress Cataloging-in-Publication Data
Dardess, George.
Meeting Islam : a guide for Christians / by George Dardess.
         p. cm. — (A many mansions book)
ISBN 1-55725-433-8
1. Islam—Relations—Christianity. 2. Christianity and other religions—Islam. 3. Islam—Doctrines. I. Title. II. Many mansions.
BP172.D3725 2005
297'.088'27—dc22   2005013504

10 9 8 7 6 5 4 3 2 1

Published by Paraclete Press
Brewster, Massachusetts
www.paracletepress.com

Printed in the United States of America.

CONTENTS

INTRODUCTION   v

INTO THE HEART OF IT

ONE *Islam* and *"Thy Will be Done"*   1

TWO *The Qur'an* and the Word of the Lord   23

BEING A MUSLIM

THREE *Salat, Taqwa,* and the Ten Virgins   45

FOUR *'Abd and Wali,* and Martha and Mary   66

FIVE *Muhammad* and The Virgin Mary   86

CELEBRATIONS

SIX *Ramadan* and Christmas (Lent and Easter Too!)   106

SEVEN *Hajj* and Easter   121

CONFLICTS

EIGHT *Jihad and Fighting the Good Fight* 140

NINE *'Isa and Jesus* 156

TEN *Tauhid and Trinity* 171

MANY YET ONE

ELEVEN *Hijab and the Veil of the Temple* 191

TWELVE *Takbir and "Hallowed be Thy Name"* 216

CONCLUSION 229

GLOSSARY 236

NOTES 242

Introduction

◆ Meeting Islam ◆

This book, like many introductions, is "about" Islam. That is, it seeks to impart basic information about Islam to an audience that is assumed to know little if anything about the subject. Or to put it another way: You will find many of the elements of what is sometimes referred to as "Islam 101" in *Meeting Islam: A Guide for Christians.*

But *Meeting Islam* is different in that it doesn't presume to be imparting this basic information in a neutral way (though I would argue that any claim to have a neutral view of anything is a chimera).

The book insists instead that this imparting of knowledge occurs in relationship, in a situation of reciprocity with the subject: hence the metaphor of "meeting." As if Islam and the reader were engaged in a human acquaintanceship, the reader testing Islam's boundaries, probing for areas of mutual agreement, hoping for but not forcing intimacy. And always open to surprise.

Yet because the title is *Meeting Islam: A Guide for Christians* rather than merely *Meeting Islam,* the imagined acquaintanceship receives an edge. *Meeting Islam* presumes a positive, but slightly distanced approach to Islam on the part of a generalized non-Muslim world. Certainly such an approach is necessary. But that is not what *Meeting Islam: A Guide for Christians* promises. *Meeting Islam* says that this acquaintanceship is being made by co-believers in the God of Abraham. So there are family connections, very warm ones. But there is also a long-standing family quarrel to reckon with. Some would call it a war. How we Christians negotiate this volatile family dynamic is critical.

So critical, in fact, that guidance is required.

I intend that this book fill such a need, as its subtitle—*A Guide for Christians*—indicates. All books about Islam are guides in one way or another, but what is unique about this one is that my own meeting of Islam and of Muslims over a fourteen-year period is used to encourage a similar effort on the part of you, the Christian reader. I'm not asking you to follow in my exact footsteps: Every Christian's meeting of Islam will be, must be, different. I'm urging you throughout this book to discover what your own meeting of Islam will be. I hope the tools and suggestions I offer you along the way are helpful ones. I encourage you to use your own experience of meeting Islam to improve these tools and suggestions so that Christians in future generations can meet Islam and Muslims with increasing under-standing and appreciation.

There are various metaphors to refine our understanding of what *meeting* Islam entails. "Passing over" is one of these metaphors. Passing over means moving beyond the limits of acquaintanceship, to an inner encounter taking place in one's own heart. Passing over goes further than tolerance, further even than friendly dialogue—proposing an actual crossing of the border into Islam. No shortcuts allowed! Passing over doesn't try to bypass the usual roadblocks of doctrinal differences and historical and present-day griev-ances. Instead, passing over tries to level the roadblocks or at least to find a path through them.

The scary thing about passing over is realizing that what will happen afterward—after the roadblocks are behind us—is a mystery. Or put more positively: Passing over involves adventure.

We pass over to the other religion in order to be changed by that religion—changed not in the sense of being converted, but in the sense of finding our own faith enhanced when we come back. So by calling "passing over" an adventure, I'm not proposing an escape from our faith but a return home to it. Yet we don't return with an attitude of superiority, as if the only purpose of passing over were to collect debating points for a more aggressive Christian apologetic. We return strengthened, more capable of "being what we are" (echoing Augustine's language for the Eucharist).

Notre Dame theologian John S. Dunne has inspired a rich contemporary reflection on passing over. Here's how he describes this unpredictable project:

> Trying to arrive at a sympathetic understanding of cultures other than one's own, lives other than one's own, religions other than one's own, are adventures of the mind which would probably not be undertaken for fear of unsettling one's confidence in one's own culture, one's own life, one's own religion. Or if one's confidence in these things were already shaken and these adventures were undertaken in order to find some new basis of certainty, they would probably be abandoned, for the divergence of the cultures and lives and religions would seem to indicate that no agreement could ever be reached on these matters. When one is no longer concerned about reaching agreement, however, and restoring confidence, but simply about attaining insight and understanding, then one can enter freely into other cultures, lives, and religions and come back to understand one's own in a new light.[i]

You are invited to "enter freely" with me into Islam under the proviso that what we are seeking is "insight and understanding" rather than "agreement and confidence." Not that agreement and confidence don't have their value. It is only that they do not have absolute value. There comes a time when, for the sake of insight and understanding, another need must be answered: The need of the mind—and of the heart and body as well—for "adventure," for a move beyond the familiar horizon of culture, self, and, in this case, religion, into the seemingly distant and even threatening region of the other. We make this adventurous move, this passing over, Dunne goes on to suggest, by "enter[ing] sympathetically into the feelings of another person, becom[ing] receptive to the images which give expression to his feelings, attain[ing] insight into those images, and then com[ing] back enriched by this insight to an understanding of one's own life which can guide one into the future."[ii]

Meeting Islam: A Guide for Christians introduces key elements of Islam into which you are invited to enter as if into the life of another person. Those elements include the language, teachings, history, and practices of the way of worship known as Islam. But more important than these elements are the people who constructed them. From this perspective, Islam is Muslims, some one billion three hundred million of them by many counts. Muslims are as varied a group as Christians are, with approximately the same proportion of saints to rogues. Like us, they too have been trying for centuries to serve the God of Abraham faithfully. Islam is the ongoing story of that service.

Yet Islam is fundamentally not a human product but a gift of God, a way of worship, given over the ages to all the communities of humankind, then cleansed and finalized in its Arabic version as handed down to the prophet Muhammad. This, at least, is the way Muslims themselves see their religion. As Christians we also must see Islam as God's gift if we are to pass over to it with "insight and understanding."

Meeting Islam as Christians we discover two encounters, one with God (as Muslims understand and worship him) and the other with Muslims themselves. This is not a theoretical exercise. When we meet Islam we put our bodies, our hearts, and our faith on the line. We have to make our own forays to our own local Islamic Centers, we have to engage deeply and openly with the way of worship practiced there, and then we have to look back at our own Christian faith through the eyes of our brother and sister Muslims. What do we see when we look through those eyes? What new insights into our Christian faith are opened to us?

I've structured each chapter to mimic the rhythm of encounter outlined above. First I'll share a story of my personal engagement with Muslims that highlights a particular teaching or practice of Islam. Then I'll explore the deeper dimensions of the teaching or practice. Then I'll look at parallel Christian teachings and practices to see what those aspects of our faith look like, now that I begin to see them with fresh, Muslim eyes. By structuring each chapter this way, I hope to give you a feeling for how your own meetings with Islam might unfold.

I've arranged the individual chapters in five sections, in an order that I feel best answers the questions Christians like yourselves are likely to have as you begin your inter-faith adventure. Part One, "Into the Heart of it," explores the fundamentals, Islam itself and the Qur'an, the Holy Book of the Muslims. Part Two, "Being a Muslim," looks at the dimensions of Muslim prayer and practice, both in their public and private dimensions, and at the Muslim in whom those dimensions were most perfectly embodied, the prophet Muhammad himself. Part Three, "Celebrations," brings us into the great Muslim gatherings, at homes and at mosques during the month of Ramadan, and at Mecca during the Hajj. Fortified by the previous chapters' positive emphasis, we'll tackle Part Four, "Conflicts," which addresses the areas where Christian and Muslim misunderstandings and differences are most painful—first Jihad, then our disagreements about Jesus and the Trinity. In Part Five, "Many Yet One," we'll meditate on the way the Hijab (the face veil Muslim women wear) and the phrase Takbir ("Let us extol him!") can act as symbols of healthy, creative tension between our religions. The fifth section leads to the Conclusion, where I'll sketch out where our meeting with Islam might lead us. The purpose of our inter-faith adventure is more than merely satisfying our private curiosity or need. Our purpose is also to is lay the groundwork for a greater flourishing of what we Christians call the Reign of God and what Muslims call salaam: fullness of life for all creatures. How does meeting Islam as Christians serve such an end?

Keeping in view the goal of passing over to Islam is important for many reasons. One of them has to be for encouragement. Interfaith adventure has its costs. We are not taking a cruise in exotic lands well-protected by tour guides. We are opening ourselves to transformation. We might get hurt. We might get lost. Many times I've wondered if I haven't, as the Qur'an puts it, "strayed from the right path." My consolation at such moments has been to remind myself that passing over is simply an expansion of the great commandment and its corollary: Love God with all your heart and your soul and your strength; and love your neighbor as yourself. To love your neighbor is to pass over into his or her skin, to walk in his or her shoes, to see out of his or her eyes. It means to experience the world and God as our neighbor does, in all its concreteness. The risk—or great opportunity—of obeying the great commandment is this: As we experience the world and God in this way, we notice with a start that our neighbor's eyes are turning in a certain direction, one we wish the neighbor would avoid altogether. We're startled because this direction is the one that puts ourselves front and center. Oh, look anywhere but there! But we're helpless. We cannot control the neighbor's choices. Sooner or later we see ourselves as our neighbor sees us. What we learn from that gaze is our reward.

◆ The Islam I Have Met ◆

Allow me to put myself through a brief inquisition. Isn't *Meeting Islam* an exercise in hubris, or at least in grandiose self-delusion? What makes me think that it's possible for any one person, let alone a Christian North American, to "meet" a faith so vast and old?—speaking of Islam only as an historical phenomenon and a present-day global reality to say nothing of its purpose and reality in the mind of God. And what about the numbers involved? Just to imagine my or anyone's "meeting" the approximately one billion three hundred million Muslims in the world is an absurdity! What about the fact that my actual meeting of Islam has been almost completely confined to the opportunities offered me in Rochester, New York?—hardly a rival to Cairo, Kabul, Riyadh, Islamabad, or Jakarta as sites where the "real Islam" might be met!

My first defense is simply to lay before my internal inquisitors the opportunities just mentioned and to ask them to consider whether those opportunities, as limited in number and scope as they have been, haven't been plenty rich enough to offer a book's worth of experiences as a resource for other adventurers.

I'm speaking of the various ways I've been connected with Rochester's Islamic Center since 1991, and especially of the friendships I've formed with the extraordinarily enlightened people who worship there. If I haven't met Islam in its entirety (begging the question whether such a thing is possible), the part I have met has shown me and many others a warm, generous face. Rochester's Islamic Center, thanks to the leadership of Dr. Muhammad Shafiq and others over the years has set a high standard of citizenship among all Rochester's communities, both religious and secular, and has modeled for us an Islam that is peaceful, open-minded, hospitable, and progressive.

So it is no accident that on the evening of September 11, 2001, a large group of Rochester's pastors and rabbis brought flowers over to the Center and stood vigil on its front steps in solidarity with their Muslim friends and in common defense against the few expressions of anti-Muslim violence that did occur. The pastors and rabbis were responding to the concrete gestures of friendship previously made to them by the members of the Center.

It is no accident either that in May 2003, Matthew Clark, the Roman Catholic Bishop of Rochester, signed a Solemn Agreement with the Center and with the other mosques of Rochester. This agreement pledged a common front against religious bigotry as well as a commitment to ongoing education in each other's faith and to joint works of charity. As far as I know, this is the first and still the only such agreement in the U.S. between a Roman Catholic diocese and the local Muslim community.

This is the Islam I have met, the Islam of Rochester, New York—an Islam committed to bringing about salaam or fruitful relationships among all God's people. Yes, I'm aware that in other places Islam does not wear so friendly a face. Perhaps in those different settings I would never have met Islam at all, or have met it in such a way as to cause me to describe the meeting very differently from the way I do here.

No meeting can be hypothetical, however. Meetings are incarnational—to use a Christian word that gives me confidence to believe that what is local in my meeting of Islam is also universal. The fact is that I met Islam where I did, through the particular people and events described in this book. But the fact is bigger than its container. Everything I have to say about Islam, while colored by the specificity of each meeting, is not confined to it, because God was present at each meeting too. And, according to the Qur'an, God is not impressed by mere grandeur and size. He "does not disdain to make a symbol even out of a gnat" (*sura* or chapter *al-bakarah* or "The Heifer," 2:26). The Qur'an insists again and again that God's *ayat* or signs are everywhere present in creation, if we would bother to look. This is Islam's own way of expressing a firm belief in the immediate and concrete as the bearer of God's word.

But my main defense against my internal inquisitors is this: While my experience of Islam has its limits, it has its strengths as well. Though initiated by my personal encounters and friendships with Muslims, my knowledge of Islam isn't confined to that. The years that have passed since I first set a timid foot in the Islamic Center have been years of intense study of Arabic and of the Qur'an. One result of that study has been that I've felt able to make my own translations (or "versions," as Muslims prefer to say) of Qur'anic verses for this book. I've also bitten into a goodly chunk of the immense body of commentary on Islam by Muslims, Christians, and others. I've followed closely the history of Muslim-Christian relations over the centuries and have kept abreast of the most recent controversies. I give talks, retreats, and classes on Islam both at home in Rochester and throughout the U.S. As an ordained Deacon in the Roman Catholic Church, I work with two interfaith groups in Rochester to plan informational sessions for both Muslims and Christians—to bring the groups together physically and to acquaint them with each other's views and struggles. In short, my commitment to meeting Islam, while centered in an unlikely place, Rochester, New York, is not therefore a narrowly personal or parochial one.

Whatever the ultimate judgment on my authority to speak about Islam, the really important question is about the book itself. How will it affect you, the reader? One of the most powerful of the early revelations to Muhammad, *sura al-zilzal* or "The Quaking" has helped me focus my own prayer for *Meeting Islam: A Guide for Christians*:

> At the day of judgment
> humankind will emerge in scattered groups
> to be shown their deeds.
> Whoever has done the tiniest bit of good will see it.
> Whoever has done the tiniest bit of evil will see it.

May my meeting Islam in Rochester become a "tiniest bit of good" for me who recount it and for you who meditate on it.

ONE *Islam* and
"Thy Will be Done"

◆ A Piece of Paper on My Dinner Plate ◆

In the winter of 1991, I sat with my wife, Peggy, comfortably at home in front of our TV watching bombs drop in splendid balloons of color over Baghdad. The War in the Gulf had begun.

As we listened to the voices of broadcasters, pundits, and generals talking jubilantly about "smart bombs" and "chicken shoots," we became more and more appalled. The war and the spectacle made out of it violated the body of Christ.

Peggy and I had both been baptized as Catholic Christians less than a decade before. The United States Catholic Bishops' pastoral letter on nuclear warfare, "The Challenge of Peace," had been published not long after that. The letter had greatly influenced our young faith, giving us the confidence to believe that as Christians we were called to seek alternatives to violence as a way of solving not only personal but international conflicts. Peggy was more committed to this search than I was during the rest of the '80s. Inspired by the workshops on nonviolence offered by Jean and Hildegard Goss-Meyer under the sponsorship of the Fellowship of Reconciliation, Peggy became an active member of the nuclear-freeze movement.

My own opportunity to respond concretely to "The Challenge of Peace" came at last, in front of the TV set. I said something like this: "What we're seeing is an outrage against the gospel of love. But I can't just blame the generals. I myself am complicitous in this, because with all my fancy education, I don't know anything about Iraq and its history. I can't even find it on the map. I don't know anything about Islam, either— or anything about these people who are being bombed in my name and with my tax money. I'm as guilty as anyone else."

All true enough, if a bit overstated. I rightfully saw that I had to be included among the generals and the others, at least to the extent that I had never taken any trouble to learn either about Iraq and its history or about Islam—or about the West's and the United States's relations with Iraq or any other country whose majority population was Muslim. I thought of myself as highly educated, had the degrees to prove it, and earned my living as a high school English teacher. In my position, I couldn't defend myself by saying, "No one ever told me I needed to know that!" My ignorance and indifference had contributed in a tiny but perhaps significant way to the ease with which the war fever had been whipped up and to the glorying in violence manifested by the politicians, the generals, and the media. So my loud declaration of complicity had its point.

Still, whether it had a point or not wouldn't matter if my behavior weren't influenced as a result. What exactly did I propose to do about my announced complicity? If I'd been cautious and more thoughtful at this stage, I might not be writing this book at all. I might have said, simply and reasonably, "I'm going to read up on this subject." I would have become better informed, and that would not have been a negligible result.

Whatever the value of a more temperate approach, that is not the one I took. Carried away by my horror at the bombing and by the histrionics of my declaration of complicity, I paused and then made the following vow: "I'm going to learn Arabic."

Saying "I'm going to learn Arabic" seemed to show I meant business, but in reality it didn't commit me to anything, since there couldn't possibly be a practical way of learning Arabic in Rochester. I'd never heard of Arabic classes being offered locally. Yet my bold statement, "I'm going to learn Arabic," hung in the air. Or perhaps it's more accurate to say that this declaration of intention had a kind of resonance that awoke echoes in subsequent occasions and events.

At first Peggy and I pursued the more moderate course, that of informing ourselves. A class on Islam was being offered as part of continuing education through a local interfaith organization. As it happened, the class was taught by the accomplished Arabist Professor Emil Homerin of the University of Rochester. Short, and as necessarily limited in scope as Emil's class was, it proved to be an excellent and indispensable initial step in overcoming my ignorance. But what would the next step be? Exactly how was one supposed to go further? Perhaps one had gone far enough! Perhaps so, but not if one had already vowed to "learn Arabic"!

Then one evening during the fall I came home from school and saw, as I got ready to sit down at the dinner table, that Peggy had put a piece of paper on my plate. The resonance I spoke of earlier had produced its first echo.

The paper was an announcement Peggy had found that day on the bulletin board of our cooperative market. It announced that Arabic lessons were to be given at our local Islamic Center for a modest fee, that the public was invited, and that the last day for sign-up was that very evening. Call the following number for more information.

If I were drawing a cartoon of my reaction to this information, I'd elongate my neck and make sweat droplets shoot from my head. Then I'd pull out my tightly buttoned collar with a hooked forefinger and put the word "Gulp!" in my speech balloon.

A thousand excuses occurred to me in a rush. I was too busy. School was very demanding, too demanding, especially during the fall. I shouldn't over work, it wouldn't be good for my health. And Arabic, from what I'd heard, was horrendously, impossibly difficult.

Peggy was eyeing me, curiously. It looked as if I would have to make that phone call. But as I approached the phone I glimpsed a ray of hope. Perhaps not all was lost. Wasn't this the last day for sign-up? Surely the places would be filled! Doesn't everyone want to learn Arabic? It was bad luck that I'd found out about the classes so late. Maybe some other time!

I called. Someone with a strange accent answered. I timidly inquired about the lessons. "Probably you're all filled up, right?" No, the person said, not at all. You're very welcome. Plenty of room. Name? Address? See you there.

On the evening of the first class, I drove across town to Rochester's Islamic Center filled with dread, as if I were heading to my execution. But while I was victim of my emotions, I was also appalled by them. Why on earth was I feeling this way? What was I expecting to happen when I walked into that boxy building with the minaret and the sickle and star on top? Did I think I was going to be jumped on by fanatics and cut to pieces? I realized to my shame how vulnerable I actually was to years of anti-Muslim propaganda. It wasn't true that I "knew nothing" of Islam. My imagination was saturated with negative images that also had their violent allure. "Islam" without my knowing it had become a symbol for "otherness"—a thing to be feared and rejected but also to be titillated by.

These images weren't my own creation, nor did they pop up overnight. They were well in place long before the War in the Gulf. For example, Dante Alighieri, in the greatest of all Christian poems, *The Divine Comedy*, completed just before the author's death in 1321—a poem I was at that point teaching regularly in my English classes—planted Muhammad far down in one of the lowest reaches of hell among the Sowers of Discord. There he is split open from chin to anus by a great demon with a bloody sword. Guts hanging out, Muhammad trudges forward round that terrace in hell reserved for unrepentant schismatics like himself. By the time his route takes him back to the demon again, the wound is healed, whereupon the demon splits him open again. The process is to be repeated into eternity.

Though seriously rattled by mental pictures like these, I managed to knock on the front door of the Center and to stand firm when it was opened. Managed, not through courage, however, but through the greater fear of having to face Peggy later if I didn't go through with it. The heavy door slowly, ominously opened. . . .

Frenzied assassins with their own bloody swords raised high on the other side?

A gentle, middle-aged man, the very first Muslim I had ever met, welcomed me with a smile. He was Dr. Muhammad Shafiq, the Center's imam and the teacher of the Arabic class. He remembered speaking with me by phone, about the class. A *barakah* (blessing) on me for coming. Would I please to take off my shoes and leave them in a cubbyhole in the foyer?

I felt ashamed at my fears as well as abashed. I hadn't even known that taking off one's shoes was mandatory. But I also felt relieved. The violent images I had been conjuring seemed to dissipate like bad air before a fresh breeze. Dr. Shafiq's warm smile and handshake put me at ease. I even began to feel eager to penetrate this mysterious place. Its mysteriousness was no longer built up of fantasy projections. The mysteriousness now had to do with fact. Here I was finally, not simply talking about Islam and looking at it from the outside through the eyes of those pretty much as ignorant as I was. Now I physically touched it: The hand of my host and teacher, Dr. Shafiq, to start with, then the hands of my classmates, mostly all Muslims, in the classroom above. Truly, I was meeting Islam for the first time, by meeting real flesh and blood Muslim people.

◆ The Root of Islam ◆

But the meeting wasn't simply social. The other students, some twenty of them, had come to the Islamic Center for a purpose or rather for purposes, all of which seemed much more clearly defined than my own.

The two other non-Muslims in the class intended to visit Egypt soon and wanted to learn at least enough Arabic to be able to find out where the nearest bathroom was in the event of an emergency. A clear and laudable goal.

For the Muslims in the class, the motive was to learn enough Arabic to be able to understand their own prayers.

I wasn't surprised to discover this. I'd already learned in Dr. Homerin's class that Arabs and Muslims are not synonymous and that only one-fifth of all Muslims speak Arabic as their native tongue. The vast majority of Muslims knew no more Arabic than I did, or what they did know they knew by rote.

Again, a clear and laudable goal, this time the goal of overcoming a deficiency in understanding the language of one's faith.

But me? What actually was my goal in studying Arabic? Something as fuzzy as assuaging a sense of complicity with my country's assault on Iraq? Or as self-serving as saving face before my wife?

I had to postpone asking such questions. Class had begun! I had my first homework assignment—that of mastering the mysterious Arabic alphabet. The confusion about my motives would have to wait.

Now I must ask you to accept a fact about me that will color the way I present my meeting Islam as a Christian throughout the rest of this book. I love words and I love languages. The stranger the word and the stranger the language the hotter my love grows. To me at that time Arabic seemed very strange. So it was love at first sight.

We all take certain tools with us when we set out on adventures. A love of languages is one of my tools. On the whole it has been very useful in my adventure in Islam, since Islam depends so much on the special beauties and characteristics of the Arabic language as they are expressed in the Arabic Qur'an. So I make no apology for my love-affair with Arabic (with all the challenges and storminesses that the phrase "love affair" implies) since, thanks to this love affair, I've been able to meet Islam with an intimacy that would have been closed to me otherwise.

For example, a loving engagement with words helps us see the very meaning of the word Islam unfold beautifully from within its triliteral root.

Yes, I know: "triliteral root" doesn't sound as if it could be a source of beauty. The first thing that comes to my mind when

I hear "triliteral root" is a textbook on dentistry. I picture a tooth that requires special clamps and forceps to extract, leaving a bloody hollow behind.

What "triliteral root" does refer to may seem at first to be a little gruesome, unless you're a lover of languages like myself. "Triliteral root" actually refers to the structuring of almost all Arabic words around a cluster of three consonants. This cluster forms the word's basic meaning. Other elements, vowels in particular, are added to the cluster to give specific meanings and to determine the cluster's part of speech.

Peering into the word Islam, we see first the triliteral root, s-l-m. The basic meaning of this cluster has to do with being safe and sound, usually as a result of treaty arrangements between previously warring parties.

So far so good. Now let's probe a little deeper for the various vowel and other additions that will give s-l-m its specific meanings.

In the form *salima*, the word—now a state-of-being verb—means "to be safe and sound." Some of the nouns derived from this verb form are: *salamun*—a treaty of peace, usually reached through an exchange of gifts or hostages; *salimun*—one who has been made safe through such a treaty; salaam—the state of safety or peace itself, as well as the greeting of peace (the familiar *assalaam aleikum*—*"peace be to you"*—used by one Muslim to another).

But the form of most interest to us is the one in which the triliteral root s-l-m becomes *aslama*, a form both causative and reflexive. It means: "to commit oneself, to pledge oneself, to hand oneself over." The sense is that we are entering into a peace treaty by making ourselves a hostage or at least by pledging something we consider precious to the person who demands it. Islam is the noun form of this verb, referring to the act of committing oneself in this way. *Muslim* is the active participle of the verb, referring to the person who makes the commitment.

That may seem like a too-large dose of technical talk. But look at the bounty of what our investigation into the s-l-m root yields so far: *Islam* and *Muslim*—the two key words to be used during our adventure—root themselves solidly in the bloody earth of the inter-tribal Bedouin conflicts that characterized life in the Arabian peninsula before the advent of God's revelations to Muhammad in the late 500's CE. Islam refers to the method for escaping the inter-tribal feuding through truces. Muslim is the one who makes the method his or her own.

But the heart of the matter, the true flowering from the root, unfolds like this: The Qur'an seizes on the s-l-m root and forces it to reach from earth to heaven. The Qur'an insists on our making our truce first and foremost with God. And the way we make that truce is Islam.

The Qur'an takes words from the Arabic cultural world that Muhammad grew up in, a world of tribal warfare, and changes the scope and meaning of those words so radically that the original meanings might seem in danger of being lost.

Yet some roots go deep, as you'll know if you've ever tried to pull out an old yew bush that's taken over your front yard or even the dandelions in your lawn. The tough conservatism of the triliteral root preserves older meanings, giving the newer ones a special density. Without the awareness of these older meanings, we're in constant danger of misunderstanding the newer ones. The words of the Qur'an carry in their roots a wide range of meaning from the tribal, Bedouin world that is simply not possible to render easily and accurately in languages that work by other systems. I am not putting Arabic on a pedestal. I'm only naming one of its distinctive qualities and then saying that when such a language is given over to God's use, as happened through the revelations to Muhammad, it has to be understood on its own terms, if we want to know what it is saying.

We can't follow the way all those tribal, Bedouin words were transformed under the pressure of God's revelation in the Qur'an, but we can trace in a deeper way the transformation that took hold of the s-l-m root. The Qur'an, still referring to treaty making, stretches the s-l-m root up to heaven to include as chief partner in the negotiation, not another person or another tribe, nor even Muhammad himself as tribal leader, but God alone. The notion of treaty making is raised to a wholly different level. What is required now is not the exchange of human or material hostages between warring tribes, but the exchange of our very self for God's mercy.

For us human beings, the reevaluation of meaning requires, in the first place, a reevaluation of what it means to be human. To be human is no longer to find our meaning within tribal allegiances. To be human is to recognize that we are, before all else, creatures or creations of God: and created not just as a physical body but as a moral and spiritual entity as well. To enter into treaty relations with God means we have to hand over to him the fullness of our human identity. The new meaning of s-l-m also reveals what was previously hidden about that identity—our utter dependence on God.

Human community must be reevaluated also. God is no longer the god of the tribe, the protector of the individual group, as against other groups with their own gods. God is the God of every person because it is God who created each one of us. As a result, we're no longer able to enlist our own god in the bargaining against or with another god within the tribal system. Just as the concept of the person opens up to include the entire physical, moral, and spiritual dimension of the human, so too does the tribal system open up to embrace what was hitherto concealed, the whole community of humankind. The part becomes the whole. The tribe is now the tribe of all tribes.

One circle of expansion leads to or reveals another. For greater still than the expansion of the human person and the human community is the expansion of what it means to be God. God is no longer the powerful protector of a particular tribal group, no longer even an irascible Father Zeus trying to hold in check a pantheon of squabbling minor deities reigning over separate tribes. (It was to such a Zeus-like figure that the word for God in Arabic, *Allah*, most often referred in the tribal system.) Those tribal gods vanish into the nothingness of human folly from which they came. God is now revealed as one. To this one God all Islam, all self-hostaging, is due.

God's power does not become greater than before. Power itself is God. We can't drive any sort of wedge, however tiny, between God and a greater boundary that contains him. God *is* the boundary and the boundary-maker. Our self-hostaging to this God must be complete, absolute, without reservation.

Yet this same God who fills the universe he has made, and who has abolished all previous gods, preserves and cherishes human liberty. If this were not so, the Qur'an's constant insistence on God's mercy would be meaningless at best or a cynical trap at worst. The treaty by which we achieve salaam or peace with God and all the rest of his creation is not forced upon us. This is why the typical translation of islam as "submission" is misleading. "Submission" suggests collapse before a superior force, a breaking of the will, and a denial of human responsibility. Nothing could be farther from the spirit of those Muslims whose islam or act of handing themselves over to God is most conscious and informed. This spirit that characterizes Islam at its truest and best—just as love characterizes Christianity at its truest and best—is dignity. For alone upon all created things God has breathed into humankind God's *ruh* or spirit.

Every Muslim is conscious of this dignity not as entitlement or as a personal achievement but as a gift that is to be honored in every way and at every moment. It is honored primarily by acts of solidarity with every other creature under God's heaven. We can see this by watching what happened to the word salaam after it was seized by God for use in the Qur'an. In the old, pre-Islamic tribal world, salaam referred to the condition between tribes after they had concluded a treaty—to an absence of hostilities, at the least; to certain gestures of mutual support at best. But now, in the Qur'an, the word opens up an entirely new world, not just a better version of a previous one. In this new world, salaam begins to share much of the meaning of another famous Semitic word, the Hebrew *shalom*: Fullness of life for all people resulting from a human order built on the principles of just relationships and of right governance of creation. Unimaginable in a tribal setting, salaam is achievable now only because of God's intervention. But will salaam actually come about? That depends on each one of us! The Qur'an is insistent on this point: that the public outcome of salaam is dependent on each individual's islam. Yet the Qur'an is equally insistent that the two, the individual and the public commitment, are inextricably bound together. There cannot be salaam without a pure act of self-rendering. There cannot be Islam for oneself alone.

True Islam enters history as the islams of individuals are lived out in community. The Qur'an provides some guidelines for the historical, communal unfolding. Foremost among these are the famous Five Pillars: Confessing one's faith in God and in Muhammad as his messenger, fasting during Ramadan, payment of the poor-tax, performing the five daily prayers, and pilgrimage or Hajj to Mecca. But Islam in its historical, communal dimension embraces as well the behaviors developed over the centuries as Muslims have continued to reflect on the revelation. These behaviors cover the gamut of righteous human possibilities, from the communal requirements of peaceful daily life as codified in Islam's rich traditions of *shari'ah* or law, to the more private requirements of inner peace with God as imagined in the equally rich tradition of Sufism or Islamic mysticism. All such activities reflect the spirit of people freely acknowledging their dependence on a being infinitely greater than themselves.

Yet that greatness must embrace all humanity. The particular revelation of God's mercy to the *ummah* or community of Muhammad does not, cannot, exhaust this mercy. In fact the Qur'an insists that this mercy was extended to all people at the dawn of human creation. And it has been revived in subsequent generations by the many prophets sent by God, beginning with Abraham. With the Arabs it was always a case of *their* "remembering" as well. For according to the Qur'an, the world didn't begin in tribal darkness. The roots of Islam push down and deep through the outer crust of Bedouin polytheism to the original strata of the Creation itself. Nor are those deepest roots confined to the Arabian desert. They spread out laterally as well. Dig down far enough, and we'll find them in Rochester, New York, and in your hometown too. How could it be otherwise, if God is the God of all creation?

Islam kept this universal sense of itself unequivocally until the early nineteenth century. Until the time, that is, when the West began to dominate Muslim lands. Until then, Muslims had referred to their way of worshipping God not as Islam—which in its substantive form occurs only eight times in the Qur'an—but as the very frequently occurring term *iman* or faith. We Westerners had referred to Islam as "the religion of Muhammad" or "Muhammadism." This grossly inaccurate term—reflecting a belief that the creator and center of Muslim worship was Muhammad himself—was rejected by Western scholars of the new science of comparative religion. The scholars sought a more accurate term for a religion they were seeking to classify according to their own scientifically based taxonomy. So they renamed the religion "Islam" on the basis of those few instances in the Qur'an where the word *islam* actually appears. The most decisive of these (for the scholars) was the following, a verse thought to be the very last one handed down to Muhammad by God:

> Today I have perfected your *din* and have fulfilled my favor towards you and have approved *islam* as your *din*. (*sura al-bakarah* 2:128)

The traditional Muslim understanding of din in this and other verses had been "way of worship," as the general name for those moral and cultic practices which the ummah or community was to abide by. Islam names those practices as characterized by self-yielding. The traditional emphasis—flowing from the special character of the Arabic language itself—was on action, behavior, and on one's internal disposition revealed and shaped by that behavior.

But as reinterpreted by the Western scholars, din no longer referred to a way of worship—to a complex of practices given to all humankind by God—but to "religion," a thing, a name, a proper noun denoting the way one group lives out that call, as distinguished from the way other groups do. In contrast to Islam's once universal application to all humankind, as a response to God being available to everyone, this new westernized Islam seems to shrink to fit human categories alone: *this* religion as opposed to *that* one. Islam as distinct religious "other" rather than Islam as humanity's response to God's gift of mercy.

Muslims did not themselves choose this shrinkage. But the pressure exerted by Western scholarship, backed by the power of Western colonizers of Muslim lands, was too great. Eventually, Muslims themselves began to use Islam in the new, restricted sense: as one religion among many—a sad fate for the rich s-l-m root whose meanings we watched proliferate transformatively in Muhammad's own time. Islam as a sign of socio-political distinction (*their* religion as opposed to *ours*) begins to crowd out all other meanings, as if the mighty s-l-m root were reduced to this one shoot only. For almost all Westerners, Islam came to mean only the religion and civilization of those "others." The sense in which the term also refers to the basic human orientation to God is lost. Lost too is a mediating sense of Islam, one that combines the universalizing sense with the effort by a particular community, the ummah of Muhammad, to understand God's call to Islam in their particular tribal world. Because each Muslim in the world today struggles with her or his Islam in a different way, it would be better to speak of Islams rather than of Islam.

If our study of the s-l-m root means anything, it informs us that this root goes down too deep and spreads too wide to be crimped and pruned into a thin little tuber supporting just another human ideology, however seductive its bloom may be to some eyes—however noxious to others. Islam is how people respond to the call of God as that call has been heard primarily, but not exclusively, through the Qur'an. Any other meaning is contingent on this primary one.

◆ How a Christian can become muslim ◆

Is the call to become a muslim one that a Christian can or should hear? There is only one way of finding out. That's by opening ourselves to the possibility and seeing what happens, confident that, however confusing the result, God will never lead us astray. Here is my own attempt to practice what I preach.

One early spring I spent eight days on retreat at Eastern Point, the Jesuit retreat house just outside Gloucester, Massachusetts. The house overlooks a picturesque bay facing the open Atlantic. Just across the lawn and through some bushes you come to an outcropping of gigantic red granite rocks that form a kind of promontory. As most retreatants at Eastern Point do, I spent hours sitting atop those rocks, watching the waves surging toward shore and crashing like thunder below me. It was an exhilarating experience. Those who have watched waves like that at some time or other will know what I mean.

But I was at Eastern Point on retreat—I wasn't there just to stare at rocks and sea. One of my missions at the retreat was to read deeply the Gospel of John.

Prayer and solitude and good spiritual direction are necessary preconditions for this kind of reading to happen. I had all three at Eastern Point. But nothing is guaranteed or forced. That is not how God works with us, if it is God whom we are seeking. Sometimes unexpected influences trigger a deepening. That happened to me.

The trigger was provided by the waves and rocks. At some point during my sitting I became aware of the extraordinary beauty in the response of those waves and rocks, and the extraordinary response of all the other natural phenomena around me, to God's will for them. The waves surged and crashed in perfect accord with nature's laws; the rocks resisted in the same way. The barnacles clung according to the laws of their own nature. Likewise the strands of seaweed lashed to and fro as the surf crashed over them. The gulls sailed above the swell or perched on rocks and dropped live mussels on them, all in accord with the laws of their natures. Everything I was looking at was acting in complete agreement with its purpose for being. And everything, even the seemingly violent things—the crashing of the surf, the occasional dead fish, birds, and other animals I saw—everything was beautiful, because everything was fulfilling its nature. Nothing was trying to be what it wasn't. Waves weren't trying to act like rocks, nor rocks like waves, nor gulls like barnacles, nor barnacles like gulls. All things in their infinite variety were one in their yielding to the laws ordained for them by God.

I don't claim that thoughts like these are original. Perhaps they occur to most people who stare at the sea as long as I did.

Then something happened that, original or not, gave the experience a different color. I found myself thinking, *Yes, all that I see is beautiful. But I need a way to sum up what makes it so. Is it rather that everything I see is muslim? That everything I see is faithfully carrying out its own islam? That everything I see has handed itself over completely to God in praise? Yes, that is why each thing acts according to its own nature and no other. That is why each thing is beautiful.*

I wasn't stretching a point. God's invitation to Islam isn't made to humankind alone. The Qur'an makes clear that the invitation was and is made universally. The Qur'an throbs with verses identifying each created thing as radiating its gratitude for that very creation. The following verse serves as well as any:

Don't you see that it is God whom all beings praise in the heavens and on earth? That the birds praise him as they wing their way? Each creature knows its own form of prayer and praise. And God knows very well what they do. (sura al-nur 24:41)

No Qur'anic verse is simply descriptive. The verse just quoted is typical. The birds aren't meant to be imagined or looked at. They're meant as ayat or signs of God's mercy. All such signs are placed throughout heaven and earth to call our attention to God. In this way the Qur'an gets moral leverage on the listener, a pressure applied in this case by interrogatives. Who is the "you" addressed at the beginning of the verse? Why does this "you" have to be addressed in such a challenging way? The Qur'an is so deeply imbued with moral challenge that it's impossible not to turn every remembered phrase in it into a mirror on one's conscience.

I say this because, soon after making the Muslim connection, I began to hear a little voice in my imagination. It was a voice that seemed to speak for the waves and the rocks. It said something like this: *You're quite right, George. We ARE muslim. And because of that, every action of ours is in accordance with the wishes of the One who made us. But that's not the question. The question is rather: What about you? How muslim are you?*

Much later on, after I'd gotten back home, I came upon a verse from the Qur'an that seemed to raise the ante of the questions raised in the previous verse:

Do they stray so far as to struggle to worship someone else than God? Even when every creature in the heavens and on the earth has pledged itself (*aslama*) to him, either willingly or not? Even when they shall all return to him? (*sura al-'imran* 3:85)

Or more loosely: What is the matter with you mortals, that unlike the supposedly "dumb" beasts—unlike the seagulls or even the barnacles clinging to the rocks—why is it that you refuse to hand yourselves over to me? Even though you have promised to do just that? Even though you know you will all return to me at death to render an account of yourselves?

I can keep questions like these at bay as long as I don't put them to myself directly. They sound safe in the verse just cited, when the question is put to all humanity and thus to no one in particular. Although the questions have that universal dimension, their primary goal is always the individual believer. This is one of the great tasks of the revelation as handed down to Muhammad's heart, to reveal and thus make real the individual's conscience, detaching it from bondage to the group ethics of the tribe and from the private designs of the ego.

My own conscience was in a vulnerable state during my retreat. Deliberately so. I was on retreat to give my conscience a good shake. I had invited the waves' and rocks' interrogation. But what was the point of their interrogation? Were the waves and the rocks asking whether I might be just too stupid or too easily distracted to hand myself over? Or were they asking whether I might be like a naughty child: told to do one thing but stubbornly insisting on doing another? Or is there something much more critical at stake in my possible refusal of Islam than bad behavior?

If the waves and rocks are muslim because they agree to be what God has asked them to be, then isn't the question about my Islam a question of my refusing to *be* what God has made me to be? Why would I do that? What *am* I supposed to be?

Back in my room at the retreat house I again picked up the Gospel of John. The waves and the rocks had aroused and directed my attention to John with renewed vigor. They seemed to give me a way of approaching this Gospel that answered my original hope, that I might enter more deeply into it. The key was to follow where the thread of Islam led me, and to do so freely and fearlessly, without worrying about the doctrinal contradictions I might stumble on along the way.

I began by acknowledging that my resistance to Islam, to handing oneself over to God, is one of the chief issues in this Gospel. For example, we're told in the very first chapter of John that "He came to what was his own, and his own people did not accept him." Again and again in this Gospel Jesus explains his message of friendship and healing to us mortals and backs that message up with a series of what the Gospel also calls "signs." (Like the Qur'an's "signs," Jesus' "signs" in the Gospel of John challenge us to recognize God's mercy.) Each time Jesus is met at the best by incomprehension and at the worst by open hostility.

We see this resistance take ominous shape beginning in the sixth chapter after the multiplication of the loaves. Here Jesus explains himself to the people and they reject his claim to be the Bread of Life.

This is a rejection of what I'm tempted to call "Christian Islam," because it is the rejection of Jesus himself. I'm tempted because, as we follow Jesus' words and actions through the Gospel of John, we discover that in Jesus himself we see what the human person is supposed to be: That in Jesus himself humanity for the first time takes its true form; and that when Jesus, later on in the Gospel of John, invites us to become his friends, he is inviting us to become what we are—united with him and the Father through the Holy Spirit in love and in unity of will. In this sense Islam leads us Christians to say, thy will be done.

Jesus' invitation led me to ask—because Islam, as I've said, always begins in the individual's heart: Why do I tend to resist yielding now that I can see so clearly the Person to whom my yielding is due? And especially now that I can see what results from not whole-heartedly giving over my will to God? It's not just a matter of being "disobedient"; it's a matter of denying my own being, like a wave which refuses to be a wave or a rock a rock or a barnacle a barnacle. It's unpleasant enough to imagine such a refusal on the part of any of these simpler creatures. How does it feel to imagine it of myself? I began to capture something beyond astonishment, something perhaps even of divine anguish in the tone of the Qur'anic verse: "Do they stray so far as to seek to worship someone else than God?"

Returning to Christianity from Islam in this way was a gratifying if exhausting feature of my Eastern Point retreat. But more relevant for the current discussion is the irony this return carried along with it. The conclusion I reached about what constitutes Christian Islam—identification with Jesus in his own self-giving—would be impossible for Muslims, even anathema to most of them. According to the Qur'an, Jesus, while a great prophet, is not in any way divine. Historically, this doctrinal difference has at times been a source of violent dispute. Proponents of both religions continue to behave badly in their characterizations of what the other has to say about Jesus. The issue can't be avoided—we'll return to it in a later chapter. For now it's enough to say, in defense of a more positive view, that the effort to think of myself as muslim, as a person striving to yield him or herself to God, has led me to engage my own Christian faith with renewed vigor. This is not, I believe, an accident. What we say in our Lord's Prayer—"Your will be done"—is a petition that Christians and Muslims can pray together. If the particular way we imagine the God to whom we give up our will—so that God's will is done, not ours—is different, that difference is not so great that it necessarily distorts the prayer for either one of us. As a Christian, I find that Islam illuminates the path towards God. It does not darken it. Despite our disputes about Jesus and other matters, it is the same God who calls us and the same God we seek.

TWO *The Qur'an*
and the Word of the Lord

◆ The Sound of the Qur'an ◆

A feeling of complicity with my country's predilection for violent solutions had brought me to the Islamic Center. A love of language had sustained me once there. But neither of these seemed to justify my staying on. It wasn't clear how my feeling of complicity was affected by my studying Arabic. As for the study itself, wasn't it all a kind of indulgence, the satisfaction of an eccentric curiosity?

For several weeks I muddled along in this way, happily enough to be sure. I enjoyed my fellow students, and I was amused by the sorts of things we were beginning to be able to say. We really could ask where the bathroom was. We could tell the taxi-driver to take us to the airport. We could discuss (briefly) the weather. And we could do all this in the past, present, and future.

And then I became aware of the prayer.

Our class met in a gathering area on the second floor above the foyer, an area that extended along the front of the Center.

The *masjid* or main prayer area itself was below us and in the back. Doors opened out from our area to the women's balcony overlooking the main space. Without actually going out on the balcony, you could see the *mihrab* or niche at the back of the masjid indicating the *qiblah* or direction of prayer toward Mecca.

Since our class met on autumn evenings, it was probably the obligatory *'asr* prayer I began to be aware of. 'Asr prayer occurs from late afternoon till just before sunset. So as the sun started setting earlier and earlier, our fixed class time began to coincide with the moveable time of 'asr prayer. Dr. Shafiq and the Muslim students were obliged to leave the class briefly so that they could say these prayers with other Muslims already gathered in the masjid below. The class would resume on their return. When I first heard the 'asr prayer from the study area above—first the *adhan* or call to prayer and then the words of the prayer itself—I found it strange, foreign, exotic. I was applying the stock adjectives that comfort us into thinking we're describing a new experience, though all we're really doing is indicating our alienation from it. Yet I wasn't any longer frightened by the sound of chanted Arabic. I knew that a human language was being used, though I had no idea what the words meant.

I don't know on what evening it happened, but during one of these prayer time-outs, while I was idly listening from the gathering area above, I suddenly realized that I actually understood some lines from the prayer. Perhaps no more than *Allahu akbar* ("God, he is beyond greatness") or the words of the *bismillah* ("In the name of Allah, the beneficent and merciful"). It didn't matter that most of the other chanted words were still opaque to me. The fact that I had understood even a tiny bit changed my attitude towards what I was hearing. What had before seemed at best pleasantly intriguing now was making a claim on me. I found myself no longer on the outside of the prayer, listening in on it, but somehow included within it, especially within its rich texture of sound. And I said to myself, echoing in form at least my earlier declaration to my wife, Peggy, that I was going to learn Arabic, "I'm going to study the Qur'an."

There were at least two key differences between this latest declaration and the earlier, rather vainglorious one. One was that the decision to study the Qur'an wasn't made to impress my wife or myself or anyone else. It articulated a desire that had been forming ever since I'd first set timid foot inside the Center two or three months before. Thanks to Dr. Homerin's class, I'd been made aware of the Qur'an's central importance in Muslim worship. This was borne out by the fact that in the Center itself Qur'anic sayings on signs, medallions, and tapestries hung on the walls of the study room and of the masjid, while well-used copies of the Qur'an could be found in bookcases and on table-tops throughout. These and other artifacts had been piquing my curiosity all along. So had Qur'anic phrases salting Dr. Shafiq's conversation in class as well as the conversation of my Muslim classmates, who were struggling to understand what the words meant. I'd become gradually aware that Salat (the word for obligatory public prayer in general) was built up of Qur'anic phrases and that key verses of the Qur'an were chanted during it. So I had been inhabiting a Qur'anic environment, or flowing along in a Qur'anic subcurrent, for some time.

The other difference from my boastful "I'm going to study Arabic," besides the subtler way in which the desire to study the Qur'an was formed, was my fear that the desire wouldn't be granted. Unlike my earlier declaration that I wanted to learn Arabic, I wasn't fooling now. My desire was formed in response to a concrete, lived situation. It wasn't mixed and mingled with the histrionics of the TV War in the Gulf.

But there was something else. This situation, this Qur'anic ambience, little as I understood of it at the time, appealed to my heart and imagination. This appeal was answered in me by joy, that special joy which I, a Christian, identify as a gift of the Holy Spirit. I was aware at the time that, doctrinally, the evocation of the Holy Spirit—as the third Person of the Trinity—had absolutely no place in my or anyone's relation to the Qur'an. The Qur'an emphatically denies Trinitarian thinking. (I'll return to this point in Chapter Ten.) Yet, doctrinally repugnant to both Christians and Muslims (for different reasons) as the connection in this case might be, I had to accept the Holy Spirit as my guide in the matter and live with the contradiction as best I could— the contradiction of discovering I was meeting Islam in terms of my own Christian self-understanding, and not out of a desire to escape that understanding or in critique of it. I felt then, and even more strongly now, that it was *because* I was a Christian that I had to open myself to Islam through the Qur'an.

Soon after this experience with the 'asr prayer, I met privately with Dr. Shafiq to ask him if there was any possiblity that a person like me could actually study the Qur'an with him or someone else at the Center. I tried to make clear what I meant by "a person like me": a Christian powerfully attracted to the Qur'an but not desiring to convert to Islam. I feared that I'd be turned down. Wouldn't Dr. Shafiq and other Muslims at the Center view my lack of interest in outright conversion as an insult? On what other basis could they accept me as a student of the Qur'an? While I felt apprehensive about my request, I also felt amused. The first time I'd made a timid petition to Dr. Shafiq, when I called the Center to ask about the Arabic class, I'd hoped that I would be turned down. Now I was hoping not to be. Irony seemed to mark each step of my meeting Islam as a Christian. Maybe God was enjoying my clumsy approach to Islam. Maybe God was eager that I enjoy that approach as well. Enjoy it in the fullest sense, not only by finding joy in it but also by bringing joy to it.

What Dr. Shafiq felt at this key moment in my meeting Islam as Christian I can only guess based on the way he responded to my request. He smiled and instantly said he'd arrange something, sure. He said that I was very welcome to study the Qur'an at the Center and that he asked Allah *subhana wa ta'ala* ("God, may he be praised and exalted") to bless me in this endeavor.

God did bless me during the two years that followed. If joy is the measure we take of our blessings, then joy, as I've said, formed the foundation of my meeting Islam as a Christian right from the beginning. That this meeting led to dilemmas and ironies only enhanced the joy, gave it point and piquancy. Very often as I sat later on with my tutor Omar in the masjid, I would look up secretly to say "thank you, thank you" to the Holy Spirit for bringing me there, as awkward and as comical as my approach sometimes was. And as unwelcome or at least as out of place as a public evocation of the Holy Spirit would be in such a setting.

Those lessons with Omar consisted of regular Saturday afternoon meetings. We would sit on the floor cross-legged at the back of the masjid with our copies of the Qur'an open on our laps. We started at the beginning and worked through most of it in our two years together, he sounding out each line, I imitating him as best I could. Omar would pause to correct my pronunciation and to help me translate. Omar used the *tartil* or strict, schoolbook style of recitation of the Qur'an's verses. Progress was very slow at first. Gradually, though, thanks to Omar's encouragement, I began to gain confidence in my capacity to give some voice to language whose power and beauty were becoming more and more clear to me.

Yes, here it was again, my love of language being roused and engaged—this time satisfied at an unimaginably higher level than the fun I'd been having with individual words and the mechanics of grammar. When it came to reading and voicing the Qur'an, I felt myself being swept up into a purer realm. Not a realm cut off entirely from the messiness I live with and contribute to daily, but a realm illuminating that messiness and providing me a way of living in it more consciously and worshipfully.

I would never have predicted that I would experience the Qur'an in this way. During Dr. Homerin's class, I'd bought a translation of the Qur'an and had tried to read it. I found it turgid, repetitive, and confusing. The language itself was an awkward pastiche of King James English. A passionate attachment to a muddle like that seemed incomprehensible to me. Only fanatics could care about such a thing, I thought, or people utterly lacking in an esthetic sense.

Now I found myself groping for an adequate parallel in my own Christian experience for the overwhelming effect the Qur'an was starting to have on me. The best parallel I could point to then as well as now was the effect of listening to Gregorian chant, or to the intoning of the Gospel in the Orthodox liturgy. Language serving transcendence.

(I wasn't aware that Muslims condemn most translations of the Qur'an for the same reasons I was experiencing. In fact, they insist on calling translations "versions," in recognition of the fact that the Qur'an really can't be translated, really cannot be rendered accurately and beautifully in other languages.)

Then, toward the end of this two-year novitiate, an event occurred that confirmed my sense of how central the beauty of language was to the full expression of Islam—or, I would argue, to the full expression of any religion.

The event occurred as I entered the masjid on one of those later Saturdays to study with Omar. I heard someone reciting the Qur'an in a completely different manner from the tartil style Omar employed. The slow cadence, the meditative pauses between each verse, the heart-breaking nasalizations (where the tongue, having reached the doubled n-consonant, retreats to the middle of the palate and lingers there as the voice breaks around it and cascades slowly into the following vowel), the extended open vowels themselves (where the voice, taking advantage of the permitted lengthening, soars up, floats suspended on its highest pitch, then, trilling, descends, the whole of this reciting a balancing of the strict rules of recitation with permitted occasions of liberty)—I felt myself listening, not so much with my ear (though the listening started there), as with my heart. All I wanted to do was to have that voice fill me.

But where was it coming from? I didn't know of anyone at the Center who chanted the Qur'an in such a brilliantly operatic way—though "operatic" connotes an emotional individualism alien to all forms of Qur'anic recitation. I quickly discovered the source: a newcomer, to be sure, surrounded by admirers like myself. He was a famous *qari* or professional Qur'an reciter from Pakistan, who was spending a few weeks at the Islamic Center to give lessons in this very form of ornamented recitation called *tajwid*.

Now I conceived yet another desire, seemingly as impossible to attain as the desire to learn Arabic or to study the Qur'an. It was to sit at the Qari's feet and learn what I could of this tajwid style of chant. So once again I timidly approached Dr. Shafiq with my request. And once again, amazingly, it was granted.

At that time, the Qari knew no English, and I knew no Urdu. (I still don't.) All we had in common was the Qur'an. But that was enough. We sat, as I'd done with Omar, cross-legged at the back of the masjid with Qur'ans in our laps. The Qari would recite a line and I would do my best to imitate what he had just created. From time to time he would correct me by repeating in tartil or strict, schoolbook style a phrase I had butchered. I dutifully repeated it in that style until I'd gotten it right before he'd allow me to imitate his transformation of the same verse through tajwid. During all such corrections, the Qari showed admirable *sabr* or patience, itself a high Islamic virtue, as I tried to make my voice resonate in places undiscovered by English and other Western languages: the middle of the palate, as well as various areas at the back of the throat that I'd never known I possessed before I came to the Center. Then I had to project the voice through its upper range without straining it and learn to negotiate trills, and to do all this in a way that enhanced my own and others' prayer. Painful as this process was at times (and painful as it is to listen to myself on the tapes I made of our sessions together), I began to discover through the Qari's teaching the way in which the Qur'an is embodied in the one who chants it, in the sense that one physically becomes the Qur'an's instrument.

Anyone who loves singing will know what I mean. But there is something more, something central to the experience of passing over to the Qur'an. The Qur'an is God's song, not ours, not even Muhammad's. To allow such a song to pass through one's own body, however imperfectly, is to discover that the instrument is transformed by the music.

I hadn't realized how deeply that transformation had been working in me until I heard the Qari's voice again several years later at an Islamic conference where he was featured. Instantly on hearing the Qari's tajwid I felt at peace, wanting only to allow that peace to penetrate me, soothing my anxieties, healing my many broken places, reviving my memory of what I already knew of God's promises even while mortifying me with the recognition of my own failures in faithfulness. Muslims call the effect *huzn* or "joyful sorrow," something like the meaning of *penthos* in the tradition of the Desert Fathers. The sound of the Qur'an initiates and shapes Islam, or self-yielding, through tears of gratitude for God's mercy.

Even a Christian like me can experience this effect.

◆ The Qur'an as the Voice of God ◆

The word *qur'an* illustrates why the chanted Qur'an has such power.

Qur'an means "a reciting" and the "thing recited" at one and the same time. That is, the object recited is inseparable from the fact of its coming into being through recitation. So huzn or joyful sorrow doesn't result just from my or any listener's being attentive to a recitation of a religious text. It's that the text is realized for us, right then and there, in the voice of the Qari and in our ears as we hear his voice.

We hear in order to remember. Or rather, our hearing is a remembering. By attending to the Qur'an or to the reciting, we are participating in the original event, when, as Muslims believe, Muhammad heard and repeated the first word handed down to him by God, which was in fact the word *Iqra'* or "Recite!" (96:1) Muslims say that in exactly the same form as Muhammad heard it and all subsequent words from God during the course of the twenty-two years in which the words came down to him as aural revelations or "auditions"—in that form he repeated or recited them, each revelation in itself a separate *qur'an*, a separate reciting. When other people heard these separate *qur'ans*, they recited them as well. Then, according to the prevailing Muslim belief, either Muhammad or more probably a scribe copied the words of the various qur'ans down. Soon after Muhammad's death in 632 CE the separate qur'ans or recitings were gathered together to form the text we know as *the* Qur'an, that is, "the reciting par excellence," the timeless revelation of God to the Arabic people in their own language.

This is the revelation of the voice of God heard through the mouth of Muhammad. This voice speaks to different segments of society, to men, to women, to Jews and to us Christians (both called "People of the Book"), to Muhammad's ummah or religious community, and sometimes directly to Muhammad himself, all in Arabic. It is a voice constantly seeking to arouse moral compunction in the listener. It does so at key moments of crisis in the life of both the ummah and of Muhammad. As the crises change over the course of Muhammad's lifetime, so too do the recitings as God responds to the crises. The recitings sent down during Muhammad's first attempt to establish the new faith in Mecca are concisely poetic in form and intensely moral and theological in content. After Muhammad's *hijrah* or emigration to Medina in 622 CE, they become more prosaic and legislative. Or put another way: From moral thunderbolts shattering the Arabs' pagan fatalism, the recitings turn into specific directives for the survival and management of the young ummah in Medina. The change reflects the swift development of the faith from an appeal to the individual conscience to a rallying and ordering of community.

While the earlier recitings tend to be especially impressive as poetry, even the later, legislative ones are compelling. The Qur'an often refers to its *i'jaz*, to the fact that it is "inimitable." And this has proven true. As an artifact of aural language, the Qur'an is of incomparable quality (a quality lost, as I've said, in translation). It is meant to be heard, like Shakespeare's plays. The words need to take shape in the mouth of the reciter and in the ear of the listener. The Qur'an comes alive as it is apprehended and responded to and absorbed, not only interiorly—into one's heart and imagination—but exteriorly too, into one's hands, feet, and tongue, in a perfect balance of mutually nurturing faith and action.

Yet to imply that the Qur'an's essence is bound up in the way it is responded to by human beings, risks obscuring what for Muslims is the central fact that the Qur'an is God's direct word to Muhammad. To focus on our response to it is to insinuate that the Qur'an depends for its realization upon human initiative or at least upon a reciprocity of initiative between God and humankind. Islam vigorously denies a divine-human interchange on such a basis of equality. But, to go to the other extreme, is the Qur'an only and literally God's word? Was Muhammad no more than a passive mouthpiece for those words? Muslims debated this point vigorously in the first centuries after prophet Muhammad's death in 632 CE. They put the debate in this form: Is the Qur'an divine? Or is it created?

The debate was eventually settled in favor of the first: The Qur'an is divine. (We can trace an analogy to the early Christian debates about the divinity of Christ and their contentious resolution at the Council of Nicea in 325 CE.) At the same time, Muslims have always pointed to evidence that the Qur'an is to some degree mediated. Tradition says, for example, that it wasn't God himself who brought the divine words to Muhammad but the angel Gabriel. The Qur'an itself states, in more than one place, that those words "came down to Muhammad's heart," not to his lips. It also says that the actual words of God reside on a "heavenly tablet" since earth cannot accommodate them. Muhammad himself is venerated by Muslims as a man of extraordinary wisdom and energy—hardly a blank slate or wax tablet.

The Qur'an has never stood alone, uninterpreted. Almost immediately after Muhammad's death a vast body of interpretation began to be built up based on *sunnah* or the norms of Muslim behavior based on Muhammad's own practice. Later, Islamic *fiqh* or jurisprudence interpreted the sunnah in changing social contexts. Islamic spirituality in all its forms, including Sufism, built upon and amplified both the Qur'an's and the sunnah's hints and prescriptions for the inner development of the soul.

At issue between Islam and Christianity isn't the fact and necessity of interpretation of their respective holy texts. What's at issue is the spirit of the interpretation. The textual and historical study of the Bible that began in Germany during the nineteenth century assumes a neutral, even a skeptical attitude towards the biblical material that was resisted by many Christian denominations (including the Catholic Church) for decades and is still resisted in many Christian circles today. Muslims have never accepted the premises of such study. They admit that the actual language of the Qur'an is a human one, "clear Arabic," as the Qur'an itself puts it. But since God himself employs this language, the result cannot be open to judgment. Since a human intelligence did not put the Qur'an together, a human intelligence cannot take it apart. All human intelligence can do is humbly attempt to understand the Qur'an's language as it applies to ever-changing human experience.

It is legitimate to say, for example, that the Qur'an addresses itself throughout to the free human will, and that it does so in order to persuade, not to crush. The Qur'an's message is a simple one: Obey God by, first, worshiping him and him alone and then by building up the ummah of worshipers through acts of justice. The reward for such Islam or self-yielding is, here on earth, a community life governed by the right relationships. And in the world to come, salaam: the perfection and perpetuation of the just community into eternity. The Qur'an paints this joyful destination in forms suited to the imagination of Bedouin Arabs: in the form of cool, refreshing rivers, of fine banquets, of attractive servants of both sexes, of melodious conversations. But, contrary to Western prejudice, no riots or orgies are to be found at these banquets. Heaven is not marked by the indulgence of desire but by its fruition. Salaam is life fully lived in the light of God.

The punishment for refusing to yield ourselves to God is equally vivid and equally open to misinterpretation. Flame and burning heat are its main features. By refusing salaam with God, the hell-bound refuses all that truly soothes and satisfies. The punishment follows from idolatry, the worship of the self. This motive is revealed at Judgment Day in its true colors, as self-negation, a perpetual and self-imposed denial of all desire, except for the desire for denial itself.

The Qur'an doesn't treat these images of heaven or hell descriptively, however. The Qur'an is not a tour book of the next life. The images are meant to arrest the attention, awaken the moral sense, and to change our behavior here and now, without delay, even as the words take shape in our mind and heart. Yet this alertness isn't at all frenzied. Far from inciting the listener to passionate behavior, the Qur'an quiets the heart by diminishing every other human concern to the primary one of recognizing God's majesty over all creation. The secondary effect is a changed perspective on that creation. We can no longer be antagonistic to or in rivalry with creation once we see that it is God's creation, not our own. Our care and concern for it should mirror God's care.

What about those calling themselves Muslims whose hearts the Qur'an seems to harden? These Muslims who use it to whip up passions and discover in the Qur'an the justification for all sorts of violence? How can a reciting which I've described as having a softening effect on the heart produce just the opposite effect in, for example, Muslim terrorists?

The only answer is to say that the Qur'an, like every other object given into human hands, is vulnerable to abuse. We'll look more closely at the Qur'an's vulnerability to abuse when we consider jihad in a later chapter. For now we need to tackle another question. Even granted that the Qur'an's original effect was to soften the heart, rather than to provoke or harden it, we could still wonder why it should continue to have that softening effect today, especially in the light of the fact that the Qur'an's content is focused so specifically on issues facing Muhammad during his own lifetime. The Qur'an was given in what was at that time a negligible part of the world, in a language and a culture confined to the deserts of Arabia, bypassed by the powerful Iranian kingdoms of the Fertile Crescent to the east and by the Byzantines to the north. Why would God have spoken to such a relatively insignificant people? And, having done so in very specific ways, how could that message continue to animate believers many centuries later, in places and cultures undreamed of by Muhammad—the United States, for example?

In other words, what besides its literary qualities would have made the Qur'an transcend boundaries of space and time? If God is truly speaking to humankind through Muhammad's mouth in the Qur'an, how do those recitings speak to the Muslims of Cairo or of Rochester, New York, today?

One answer lies in what's already been said about the intensely moral light that the Qur'an throws on the listener's conscience, awakening it either to assent to the divine voice or to reject it. But another way to address the question about the Qur'an's universality is to point out that the Qur'an, while seeing its particular linguistic form as inimitable by humankind, does not regard its own message as unique, except in so far as it is a message directed to Arabs in their own language. For the Qur'an makes it clear that there was never a time when God wasn't sending this same message to humankind across the vast gulf that separates us, either through natural signs or through the words and actions of prophets like Muhammad. In each case, God adapted the form of the message to our particular conditions and understandings and languages. But the message remains the same, whether Moses pronounces it—or Jesus, whom Muslims regard as one of the greatest of the prophets. (More on Muslim attitudes towards Jesus in a later chapter.)

The Qur'an is characteristically vivid and concrete on this point. The timelessness of its message is not conceived in abstract terms, as if it were an impersonal natural law. Its timelessness is itself an act of revelation. The opening moment of this revelation occurred while we were all, the entire panorama of us through time, still sleeping as seeds within Adam and Eve. Then all at once our dreaming of our lives to come was broken by the divine summons:

> Your Lord brought forth descendants from the seeds of Adam's children [i.e. every single one of us who was ever to be] and made them testify against themselves. He said: "Am I not your Lord?" They replied: "Yes! We bear witness that you are." This God did, lest you should say on the Day of Resurrection: "We had no knowledge of that!" or "Our forefathers were, indeed, idolaters; but will you destroy us, their descendants, on account of what the followers of falsehood did?" (*sura al-a'raf* 7:172-3)

The point of these famous verses (referred to by Muslims as the *Alastu*, the Arabic word for "Am I not . . ?") is that none of us mortals ever could or ever can claim ignorance of the urgent appeal God has always been making to our moral understanding. Given our previous assent, our subsequent failure to acknowledge God's mastery and to direct our behavior accordingly is unequivocal and unmitigated disaster for us at Judgment Day. Our crime amounts to oath breaking if not treason. To prevent our becoming completely swallowed up by this moral disaster, God sends down the signs and the prophets, of whom Muhammad is the *khatamu* or "seal" (*sura al-ahzab* 33:40), a word universally understood by Muslims to mean not only the final one but the greatest.

So the Qur'an's appeal to our time has to do with its prior claim on all time, on all human time, that is. The claim on the Arabs is but the last in a series of what the Qur'an calls "reminders." In fact, the Qur'an often refers to itself as the "Reminder" par excellence, calling our wandering attentions back to commitments made while we were still dreaming in the seed of Adam. According to the Qur'an, we were never "innocent." We always were and still are responsible for what we promised, regardless of apparently mitigating circumstances and unforeseen changes to come. The message is eternal, "inscribed on an imperishable tablet" (sura al-buruj 85:22), and given to us in the very womb of time.

But there is another quality of the Qur'an not yet specified, another claim to its hold over the Muslims of Islamabad, of Cairo, of Rochester, New York, and of cities yet to be built. A quality that separates it from all other religious scriptures, over other claimants to be God's word, over even our own New Testament, and a quality that places it on a kind of timeless pedestal, safe from tampering and decay, truly "inimitable" not only as literary work but as divine communication.

This quality is rooted again in the Qur'an's nature as the reciting of God's very words. Directed as those words clearly are to the lives and language of Muhammad and his community, they nevertheless bear, according to Muslims, an eternal message in uncorrupted speech. Central to the Qur'an's status as a religion is its claim that it and it alone, of all the messages sent to the many prophets, remains absolutely truthful to God's exact intent. All other previous messages sent down to previous prophets have exactly the same content as the Qur'an: Be faithful to God and be good *khalifa* or stewards of God's creation. But in each case the message was twisted, the Qur'an asserts, by the ideological interests, not of the prophet, but of his followers. Jews bent God's desire to bring mercy to all humankind into a partisan mission in favor of the Jews themselves. Christians made an idol out of the prophet Jesus, attributing the power and mercy of God to a mere human being, great as that human being was. So it has gone with the multitude of other messages conveyed in various ways to every community that ever walked the earth. To the Arabs—not through any special excellence of their own but through God's mercy to all humankind—came the honor of being that ummah which was to receive the message in an uncorrupted and incorruptible form. What God spoke through Muhammad has been kept intact, just as Muhammad heard it. And so, Muslims say, it may be trusted, and must be trusted, by all those in subsequent ages who seek to know God's true intentions for humankind—who seek to remember the original question posed to them ages ago, "Am I not your Lord?" so that they might fulfill the promise they made when they said, "We bear witness that you are." The Qur'an clarifies how that promise is to be lived out, by all peoples' honoring God and God alone, and by doing so as one great ummah of all humankind, united despite their many differences in Islam or self-yielding to the One God.

◆ Caring For The Word ◆

Not long ago I proclaimed the Gospel, in my role as Deacon of the Mass, at a diocesan event in Rochester. I stayed around afterward to chat. A man from the congregation approached me to compliment me on my proclamation. "I could hear every syllable, and that's not easy in this church with its bad acoustics. But there was also something about the cadence that worked well, I'm not sure why."

My first impulse was to thank the man with appropriate but probably not quite sincere modesty. My second impulse was to tell the truth as I understood it. Something about the man made me want to risk the truthful version. I said, "If what you say is true, I mean if my proclaiming had any merit, it's because I was proclaiming the Gospel as if it were the Qur'an."

The man looked surprised, of course, but when I said a few things in explanation he seemed to understand, and graciously took his leave. (Or, more likely, the "few things" I think I offered actually turned into a disquisition and the man simply sought an escape!)

What I think I said to him was something like this: "See, for Muslims, to say 'Word of the Lord' is to mean exactly that, that you're using something like the very words that came to Muhammad from God. And that they are just as much God's words now as they were when Muhammad first heard them. So we have to say our own Word of the Lord with a similar reverence, not slur it or toss it off to get to something more important. So when I proclaim the Gospel, I try to treat it as if its words really are from God, which of course they are!"

I hope my reply was that short, but the downside is that, if so, it must have glossed over the important difference between the way Muslims view the inspired Word of God and the way Catholics and other mainline Christians view it. For Muslims, that Word was given directly to one human being, Muhammad. Christians, and some Muslims too, continue to puzzle over exactly how to understand the word "directly" as used of the divine *wahy* or communication.

But there is a difference in degree if not in kind between the wahy or communication given to Muhammad over the course of twenty-two years and that given to the understandings of the biblical communities who over centuries assembled the Bible's various books from various inspired materials. We mainline Christians see our Scripture as mediated: as inspired, yes, but in a more indirect sense. It is the work of many people and many communities, not of one man alone.

Emphasizing inspiration as mediated can lead to diminishing it, unfortunately. The very sophistication of Western historical understanding can give the impression that our Scripture is nothing but a mediation, nothing but a fallible human document. We acknowledge the fact that the exact words of our founder, Jesus Christ, are almost completely lost to us and that during his lifetime no one thought to record more than a couple of his words verbatim. Jesus himself never wrote a book, not even a book recording the kind of conversations he must have had with God during prayer. Furthermore, Jesus spoke, almost certainly, in Aramaic, while the various writings collected about him long after his death were produced in a different language, Greek, a language that he may or may not have understood. We Christians have always depended upon translations of those Greek writings, translations that vary in quality and accuracy and that must always be updated as the vernaculars in which they appear inevitably change. So our Christian connection to the Word of God—compared to the less mediated sense in which the Muslims regard the words of the Qur'an—might seem tenuous and uncertain.

Yet this impression of disconnectedness forgets or ignores Christian tradition. Beginning with the Desert Fathers and Mothers, Christians have dwelt deeply in Scripture through *lectio divina*, or "divine reading," the prayerful opening of the heart to the biblical word. The liturgies of the Eastern churches have never lost or given up the chanting of the Gospel. We have the testimonies to the concrete power of God's word from Jeremiah and Ezekiel, both of whom "ate" that word (Jer. 15:16; Ezek. 3:3); and from Jesus himself, quoting Deuteronomy, who said: "One does not live on bread alone, but on every word that comes from the mouth of God" (Mt. 4:4). We Christians don't have to look with envy at Muslims whose appreciation for Scripture as the living word of God seems at times far more vigorous than our own. Our own tradition validates this appreciation. For Roman Catholics, this appreciation was reinforced in the Second Vatican Council's "Dei Verbum" (or "The Dogmatic Constitution on Divine Revelation"). Among other things Dei Verbum asserts that in our Scripture

> God, who spoke of old, uninterruptedly converses with the Bride of His Beloved Son; and the Holy Spirit, through whom the living voice of the gospel resounds in the Church, and through her, in the world, leads unto all truth those who believe and make the word of Christ dwell abundantly in them.

And of course, we Christians understand Word of God in a way in which Muslims do not, as the Logos, the second Person of the Trinity, the Son in whom we die and rise again through the Holy Spirit. So when we listen to the Word of God as proclaimed from our pulpits, we aren't relying on the actual words themselves to embody God's presence. We rely on the Holy Spirit to help us hear Christ's voice speaking to us through those words. In the liturgical Christian churches, the hearing of Christ's voice prepares us to receive him bodily, in the Holy Eucharist that follows. As a single liturgical action, the Eucharistic celebration puts us in a relation to the proclaimed word analogous to that of a Muslim responding with huzn or penthos, joyful sorrow, to the chanted words of the Qur'an, especially as those words are heard in salat or public prayer.

So while a fully liturgical understanding of Word puts a gulf of difference between Christianity and Islam on one side, on another a wonderful congruence—though not an equivalence!—is revealed. As symbols of the communal celebration of the word in both religions, the Qur'an is more adequately compared with the Eucharist itself than with the Bible. In both the Qur'an and Eucharist God shares with us God's self through the word. Both Qur'an and Eucharist put us bodily in God's presence and make an overwhelmingly immediate appeal to us as individuals and as communities to turn all concerns and attachments over to Him who alone exists, who alone is great.

How ironic that the Qur'an opens our Christian eyes more fully to what the Qur'an itself denies, that Christ is Lord!

Thanks be to our Muslim friends for reminding us of what is central to our own faith and of the importance of the proclaimed word in arousing and sustaining it.

THREE Salat, Taqwa, and the Ten Virgins

◆ Learning to Pray Like a Muslim ◆

In 1995 I published an essay in *Commonweal* magazine entitled "When a Christian Chants the Qur'an." The essay described the dilemma I found myself in when Dr. Shafiq invited me to join him and the other Muslim men in the prayer line at 'asr (evening) prayer.

Dr. Shafiq made the invitation quite casually one Saturday afternoon after I'd been coming to the Center for at least a year. Dr. Shafiq wasn't putting any pressure on me to accept the invitation. Nor was he asking me to take the first steps in renouncing my own religion by doing so. He took very seriously God's word in the Qur'an, "Let there be no compulsion in ways of worship" (*sura al-bakarah* 2:256). He was acting on the Qur'anic principle that Islam is a universal religion, to which all monotheists, including Christians and Jews, are invited. My joining the prayer line would mean no more, as far as he was concerned, than that I visibly and communally assented to that principle.

And I did assent to it! The beauty of the Qur'an and the warmth of the friendships I'd been making at the Islamic Center made me want to stand shoulder to shoulder with Dr. Shafiq and the others at the Center in order to enact physically and liturgically what I already embraced in my heart—not only Islam or self-yielding to Allah ("Allah" is the word for "God" in Arabic—the same God whom all Christians and Jews worship), but also solidarity with all those others who have embraced Islam throughout the ages. The Qur'an, the Holy Book of the Muslims, had taught me that this human embrace extended to those outside the ummah of Muhammad. Yet there was an embrace incomparably wider still. This embrace was God's own. All created things were gathered up in it. It was hard to see how I could separate myself from an embrace larger than my own or even than all humanity's, one that included me within the sweep of all that ever was or was to be.

Yet Islam in this sense, a basic and universal orientation towards God's *rahmat* or mercy, was one thing. Islam as the way a specific community expresses that orientation was another. I assented wholeheartedly to the first, but to the second I couldn't assent because of the obvious barrier of my prior commitment to Christianity. This barrier was indeed large. How could I in good conscience line up with the other men at prayer and thus give every signal to them that my primary communal allegiance was to the ummah of Muhammad when in fact my allegiance lay elsewhere—to what a Muslim friend once described as the ummah of Jesus, my own Christian community, in both its local and universal manifestations? What kind of signal would I be giving to them? To join the prayer line seemed to me a betrayal of the trust of both communities, not only of the Muslim but of the Christian as well.

Of course, I could have said that allegiance to God's call to unity overrode my allegiance to a particular community and the faith that nurtured it. Buoyed up by that idealism, I could have vaulted into the prayer line without a qualm. But I rebelled against what seemed to me a too-easy dismissal of Christian and Muslim differences. God calls all his creatures to unity, I had no doubt of that, but this call is no mere theoretical insight, no mere logical deduction that forces compliance. Nor is it a sentimental sop thrown to our desire to feel warm and pure inside by pretending our differences have no truth to them. The call to unity always comes through particular circumstances and relationships. It is always embodied in the way we live our lives and in the people with whom we live them at a particular time and place. Those lives and those people are always spikey and difficult.

But this is what I had to admit: As much as I valued unity, I valued the spikiness and difficulty of difference just as much. In fact, I couldn't—and still can't—separate the one from the other.

So while I longed to join Dr. Shafiq and the others in prayer, I found I could not do so. I would be saying, it seemed to me, that the differences between our faiths don't really matter, that they are pitiful illusions that those of a higher intelligence ought to be able to discard. Even if the differences really were illusions, it was for God, not any of his creatures, to reveal them as such.

Resistant as I was—and still am—to a too-easy blending of our religions, I still didn't consider my not joining the prayer line a refusal of Islam. Refusal implied greater certainty about the exact nature of my relation to Islam than I possessed. I felt rather that by declining Dr. Shafiq's invitation I was putting myself in a state of suspension, or even in suspense, if one takes away the negative connotations of the word suspense. I had to wait. I had to resist grasping impatiently for a solution to my dilemma. Instead, I had to put my needs and desires on hold for a while. Sometimes I likened this period to a kind of fasting. At other times I likened it to the months prior to my baptism as an adult in 1983: a difficult but graced time of joyful expectation. Then as now I felt that there was a special joy in *not* being gratified in the way I longed to be, by joining the men in prayer. I didn't want to endanger that joy by a premature rush for resolution.

Writing the *Commonweal* article did not solve my dilemma, but it did help me mark a stage in my relation with Islam. By writing it, I was able to look back at the events that had brought me to my dilemma. Writing it also gave me a way of proposing a future. In that future, I might never be able to join the prayer line, but I could be on the watch for hints of other and perhaps more suitable ways I might express both my commitment to Islam in the universal sense and my solidarity with Islam in the communal sense, as the specific practice of the ummah of Muhammad. I couldn't know at the moment what those hints might be, but I felt sure that, given the dramatic, unexpected, and sometimes comic way in which my relation with Islam, in both dimensions, had been unfolding so far, there were more stages and dilemmas to come.

In the meantime, what to do? A thought began forming in me.

Nothing was stopping me from at least learning how to do Salat, the embodied liturgical prayer of Muslims. I had watched it often enough from my position at the back of the masjid. Surely there was no harm in rehearsing its steps, in putting my body and my voice through the process so that, if it ever happened that I could feel free to do Salat in earnest, I wouldn't have to stumble through it. After all, if I, a Christian, was learning to read the Qur'an in the Muslim manner, I ought to be able to worship in the Muslim manner also. In a preliminary, non-committal way, of course!

I knew that such reasoning was specious. I knew that liturgy is not playacting. I knew that going through the motions of prayer without actually intending to pray is risky business. Wouldn't I be flirting with hypocrisy? Maybe even courting disbelief?

The analogy between learning the Qur'an and learning the prayer of Salat struck me as shaky as well. Learning the Qur'an, whatever its risks to my Christian commitment, did not at least draw me into Islam's communal dimension, a dimension usually defined in terms of Islam's Five Pillars: *Shahadah* (confession that there is no God but God and that Muhammad is his prophet), *Salat, Zakat* (regular almsgiving), *Sawm* (fasting, especially during Ramadan), and Hajj (pilgrimage to Mecca). The external, public dimension of religious life plays a more important role in Islam than it does in Christianity. In fact, one of Islam's traditional criticisms of Christianity is that Christianity is overly spiritualized: that it does not assert itself comprehensively over all aspects of the life of the ummah of Jesus as Islam does over the life of the ummah of Muhammad.

The upshot of my doubts was a growing suspicion that by trying to play the role of a Muslim at prayer, I was proposing a kind of behavior that could backfire, could lead me into deep waters where I was not prepared to swim.

I dove in anyway.

I asked Dr. Shafiq one day if he could lead me through the motions and prayers of Salat. At least I didn't encumber him with my doubts. The negative consequences of my decision, whatever they might be, should fall on my conscience, not his.

So on an occasion when we found ourselves alone at the Center, he brought me into the masjid and guided me through the positions. He didn't put me through the necessary first step, called *wudu* or the ritual washing of hands, mouth, nostrils, face, arms, ears, neck, and feet, in that order. He started out in the second stage, in the masjid itself, by having me stand side by side with him, feet slightly apart, facing the qiblah or the direction to Mecca. We raised our hands to our ears, symbolizing our *niyya* or intention to concentrate our minds and hearts on God, and said *Allahu akbar* ("God, there is none greater"). With the right hand placed on the abdomen and the left hand covering it, we recited together the most important of Salat's prayers, the *fatihah* or "Opening." Then we performed the key action of public prayer, *sujud*, sometimes—misleadingly—translated as "prostration."

I say misleadingly because the sequence that Dr. Shafiq then asked me to follow is not prostration at all. To prostrate oneself is to lay face down flat on the floor—to become completely passive, as a sign, perhaps, of our utter powerlessness before an overwhelming force. By contrast, sujud requires a practiced flexing of different parts of our body. And our body is almost constantly in motion. It pauses at each part of the sequence only long enough to bring a particular posture into focus, then resumes a cycle that consists of the following steps: bowing from the waist, standing upright again, kneeling in place, sitting back on one's heels, leaning forward till forehead, nose, and hands touch the carpet, moving back into a sitting position with the right leg bent straight back and the left bent underneath the body, then rising to an upright position again by rocking back on one's heels.

Not an easy series of maneuvers! As I followed Dr Shafiq's lead, I could tell that various parts of my body were getting a healthy stretch, especially during the beginning stages of sujud, that is, up to the point where I touched my forehead on the carpet. After that, though, I found that other parts of my body, like my ankles and knees, were beginning to scream in protest. Dr. Shafiq chuckled, not unkindly, to see me struggle afterwards to bend my legs under me (I didn't succeed). He had another laugh when he saw I couldn't complete the sujud by rocking back on my heels and coming to a standing position in one motion. I chuckled ruefully as well.

It wasn't just the athleticism involved in sujud that distanced it from prostration—it was the way the accompanying liturgical prayers that Dr. Shafiq also taught me to say gave meaning to the motions. Those prayers reverence God and give thanks to him for his rahmat or mercy.

I'll give some of those prayers here so that the next time you're observing Salat at your local mosque you'll realize there's nothing outlandish about this practice at all. You might even be tempted, as I have been, to join in!

As the people begin to bow down you'll hear them say, "*Allahu akbar!* (God, there is none greater)." Then, placing hands on their knees, "*Subhana rabbiyal 'azim* (Glory to my Lord, the Almighty)." Standing up from the bowing position, "*Sami' Allahu liman hamidah* (Allah hears those who praise him)". These phrases are repeated throughout the prostration and the final standing to complete one *rak'ah* or unit of Salat.

Nothing about these prayers suggests that any Muslim is expected to feel reduced to an inert mass or abject slave trembling before a tyrant. Rather, Salat as embodied liturgical prayer expresses at once dependence and independence, self-yielding and self-possession, giving-over and taking-up as poles or opposite moments of the appropriate human response to God's appeal. No one posture can be subtracted from the totality of this response, either to be discarded or to be exaggerated at the expense of the others. If touching the forehead to the floor expresses the extreme of dependence, standing up again asserts human dignity, for did not God uniquely bestow on humankind his ruh or breath/spirit? (*sura al-hijr* 15:29)

How did all of this look from God's side? If thanks to Dr. Shafiq's tutelage I had a better feel for the way Muslims sought to embody their islam or self-yielding, where—if it made sense to put it that way—was God standing?

One of Dr. Shafiq's comments during our tutoring session opened up an answer. "When you are doing *qiyam* or standing," he said, "you gaze at that spot on the carpet where you will be putting your forehead. Because when you put your forehead there, you will be putting it right before the feet of God."

God was that breathtakingly close! I had somehow, and wrongly, imagined him as infinitely distant, like a potentate seated on a throne. But no: he was right in front of me, his feet, so to speak, just an inch from the crown of my head: not encroaching on the space reserved for my sujud, and even allowing me to establish the proper distance, but nevertheless—as pictured in a famous *ayah* or line from the Qur'an—"as close as your jugular vein" (*sura qaf* 50:16).

Dr. Shafiq's comment acted as a catalyst on the somewhat scattered impressions I'd had about Salat up till that moment.

Clearly Salat required a communal commitment and a very physical, almost athletic practice. But just as clearly Salat couldn't be reduced to its communal and physical components. For if Salat took place horizontally, as an activity carried out in concert with others, it took place vertically also, as inward response to the divine closeness Dr. Shafiq had drawn my attention to. The divine closeness was the initiating impulse of Salat. Not simply a part of Salat, but what made Salat possible and necessary for those who responded to it, first inwardly, then communally, in the forms of the sujud I'd just painfully been taken through.

Would I have been able to glimpse these connections if I hadn't been moving physically through the prayer? I'm inclined to think not. Whatever the dangers inherent in my playacting of Salat, there was at least this reward: a sudden but tranquil intimation of how coherently Salat embodied both the outer and inner dimensions of Islam.

◆ The Importance of Taqwa ◆

Salat, prayed publicly five times a day between one day's dawn and the next, makes spatial direction concrete along two axes. Along one axis, the men and women of the ummah of Muhammad line up in parallel rows. There are no privileged places in these rows. Each worshiper joins the row at the available spot, filling in the rows from the front. He or she stands shoulder to shoulder with his or her neighbor, allowing no room for *Shaitan* (Satan the deceiver, the whisperer) to slide between. The fact that women and men perform Salat in different spaces in the masjid doesn't violate the basic egalitarianism of the arrangement. (More on this last point in Chapter Eleven.)

This axis is crossed at right angles by another horizontal one. This second axis passes through the qiblah or niche at the front of the masjid and stretches towards the Ka'bah, the square stone structure in Mecca held to be the site of creation, of the Garden of Eden, and of the place of sacrifice built by Abraham and Ishmael. Muslim prayer is literally concentrated around that point. All around the world the one billion three hundred million Muslims, including my friends in Rochester's Islamic Center, form sections of concentric circles made up of all the prayer rows that constantly form and reform as specific points are passed in the sun's journey across the sky from dawn to sunset to dark.

Yet these two horizontal axes, powerfully drawn as they are through space and time, reveal only dependent dimensions. Take the axis orienting all bodies and hearts towards Mecca. True, the Ka'bah is the center of Allah's revelation. But the worshipers are not bowing down to the stone structure, nor even to the memory of the great events of faith associated with it. And while the physical unity of the ummah of Muhammad is reaffirmed again and again by each performance of Salat, group belonging is not at Islam's heart. The word *islam* itself—which occurs only eight times in the Qur'an—is not adequate to denote what is at that heart. The word used far more often in the Qur'an to identify the inner spring of response to God's appeal to humankind is *iman* or faith. The word used to measure the adequacy of each person's iman is taqwa or attentiveness.

Taqwa comes from a root that means "to guard, to keep oneself (or someone else) safe, to protect." As a concrete noun, it refers to a "shield, a device for warding off." In Bedouin context, that is, in the imaginations of the nomadic desert tribes to whom Muhammad proclaimed the Qur'an's or recitings he'd received from God, taqwa meant being alert and armed against attack, on the defense.

What we have to imagine is something like this: The time is the middle of the sixth century of the Common Era. The place is somewhere in the desert of the Arabian Peninsula. The time is nightfall. We are shepherds from a particular tribe who have just finished bedding down our flocks near one of our tribe's precious oases. We're on patrol throughout the starry desert night, carrying a torch in one hand and a shield on the opposite arm. We listen to the night sounds. We fight off drowsiness. We know that our own lives, the lives of the sleeping members of our tribe, and our livelihood—our flocks—depend on our alertness. We know that there is great danger out there in the darkness from wild animals. But the deadliest danger we face is from other tribes. That's because stealing each other's property is a way of life among all of us.

That is the behavioral, external meaning of taqwa. The word carries a secondary meaning of "to fear." Not fear in the sense of panic, but as the concern that comes from an acute sense of responsibility—being supremely awake through dedicated effort. Being constantly on the tips of one's toes. Being constantly poised. With this secondary meaning we enter the moral realm. Yet in Qur'anic Arabic, moral values aren't expressed as abstractions but as actions. The inner disposition of alert responsibility can't be separated from the manifesting of the disposition in one's life, in one's deeds.

The characteristic transformation exerted by the Qur'an on words denoting old Arab virtues, like taqwa, is to detach them from their tribal settings and to orient them strictly and solely to Allah. We saw a similar transformation happen with the word *islam*. By an analogous process the word "Allah" undergoes transformation. From a word denoting the supreme god (like Zeus in the Greek pantheon), Allah (which literally means "the god") now rules absolutely alone. Gone are the multiple deities and the wavering moral compass of the *jahiliyya* or "time of ignorance," the word used in the Qur'an to refer to the state of moral affairs among the pre-Qur'anic Bedouins. In that "ignorant" time, rival gods exerted competing demands of loyalty and virtuous behavior on their particular tribes. Morality cemented tribal solidarity over against the other tribes. No longer! All demands now issue from just one source, and because of that, the divided and competing tribes become one. There emerges a unified focus on the moral level as well. Taqwa points in such a powerful way towards this single source of divine power, Allah, that the other transformed virtues are subsidiary to it. Alertness to Allah's commands and to the temptations that could keep a person from following those commands now takes center stage.

The predominance of taqwa in the Qur'anic system surprised me when I first became aware of it, because I was slow to realize how profoundly the Qur'an had reversed and transformed all previous values. In the jahiliyya, the actively martial virtues were the ones celebrated. Now, after the revelation to Muhammad, it is the negative, defensive stance that receives pride of place. As I thought about it further, I saw why the shift of value had occurred. Islam or self-yielding to God leaves no room for competing egos. The new moral life begins with the recognition of our utter insignificance before the Lord of the worlds. Human beings, in this new dispensation, have nothing to brag about, as they once thought they did in their jahl or ignorance, when they lorded it over other tribal lordlings. Rather, the true human destiny is to become servants or *'abad* of the Lord, in gratitude for his bounty. Taqwa reflects our acute consciousness of the overwhelming asymmetry of our relation to Allah. Though acute, this consciousness is never crushing. Mostly that's because Allah is *rahim*, supremely merciful.

Yet taqwa itself asserts an inner equilibrium. The equilibrium was visible even during the jahaliyya. Being poised and alert around the Bedouin campfire implied that, for sure, enemies might be on the prowl. But it also implied that friends might be out there too. When friends arrived, we dropped our shield and we embraced those friends. Vital to taqwa in the jahaliyya sense was, then, a heightened capacity to distinguish friend from enemy. Islamicized, taqwa includes a heightened sense both of what pulls us away from Allah and of what draws us closer. The moral equipoise suggested here is what the great Islamic scholar Fazlur Rahman is getting at when he defines taqwa as "a unique balance of integrative moral action."[iii] Taqwa, Rahman says, highlights the fundamental orientation of Islam towards the mean between extremes (pride and hopelessness, freedom and determinism, asceticism and profligacy, individualism and communalism, etc.). For this reason, taqwa is very much what Rahman calls a "torch"[iv] to help the Muslim decide between right and wrong, an "inner light, a spiritual guide."[v]

But a guide through what? I began wondering about the source of the urgency or "fear" that motivates taqwa in this new Islamicized sense of things. I could understand the urgency motivating the caravan sentry. Those are not theoretical lions and marauders out there in the darkness. Those lions have fangs and claws, and the marauders real swords. Our lives are in the balance. Our necks are sticking out. But for the Muslim? What is "out there" that he fears?

Here is where the Islamization of the old Bedouin values is perhaps most obvious. Taqwa is no longer focused on external enemies, but rather inwardly, on the management of our own will. Taqwa is conscience, but conscience energized by the Qur'anic revelation of the divine *amr* or command. Taqwa seeks constantly to align the amr of God (perceived as consistently and unwaveringly benign) with the inconsistent and wavering condition of our hearts. Taqwa's goal is to stabilize our hearts, to allow them to beat at a healthy rhythm. The consequences of not doing all we can to maintain that rhythm are fatal to a degree unimaginable in the jahaliyya. That's because the Qur'an introduces to the old Arabic world an entirely new reality: Judgment and life after death.

Placed before this newly revealed future, Muslims see themselves in mortal and spiritual crisis at each instant. This is the function of the Qur'an's many warnings of the imminent Day of Judgment. Muslims live, so to speak, in constant and unremitting sujud—as if during every second that life lasts they are standing and preparing to bow down at the feet of Allah, spreading out their hearts and their deeds to God's view. Salat is a rehearsal for the Day of Judgment. On that day, every atom's weight of good and evil that we do will be laid bare (*sura al-zilzal* 99:7-8). Nothing will be hidden any longer, no excuses and special pleadings allowed. Yet judgment will not be pronounced on us by an avenging deity. Our very skins will convict us:

On that Day the enemies of God will be gathered together for the Fire, they will be marched along in ranks

And once they reach the Fire, their ears, their eyes, their very skins will testify against them about all those things they used to do.

The sinners will say to their skins, "Why are you testifying against us?"

Their skins will reply: "God, who gives all things speech, has given us speech as well. He created you at the beginning, and to him you were always to return.

"You never thought about hiding your evil from us so that we could not testify against you. And you imagined that God would not know about the worst of your deeds. But this fantasy you dreamt up about your God has brought you to the brink, and now your only companions are those who are utterly lost." (*sura fussilat* 41:19-23)

The vivid language of such passages is often misinterpreted, not only by many Westerners but by Muslim extremists too. Both groups tend to read the Qur'an's strong images of fiery damnation as well as of sensuous heavenly delights literally, as if life after death amounted to little more than one's own self-gratification or the utter confounding of enemies. The judgment, however, is God's, not ours, because only Allah can read human hearts. Allah does so, not by mulling over our cases like a human judge employing human and therefore imperfect law. Allah does so by bringing us into a position after death where all is light. In that utter clarity, the murkiness of human motive dissolves once and for all. What we have done (inseparable from how we have done it) stands out in excruciating detail. Have we praised God with a sincere and undivided heart? Have we put this praise in practice by dealing with each other with a mercy like God's own? These are ultimate questions for which taqwa is meant to prepare us here and now.

May our ears, eyes, and skin never have reason to testify against us! May taqwa guide us while there is still time!

◆ Returning to the Ten Virgins ◆

Ordinarily, I study and meditate on the Sunday readings before I go to Mass. But on one particular Sunday a few years ago, I hadn't had the chance to do so. I felt a little guilty for the omission, I must admit, and felt obliged, by way of compensation, to be especially attentive to the proclamation. It would give me my only opportunity to reflect on the Word before the homily began.

The Gospel reading for that day was Luke 12:32–48, in which Jesus builds images of watchfulness:

> Be dressed for action and have your lamps lit; be like those who are waiting for their master to return from the wedding banquet, so that they may open the door for him as soon as he comes and knocks.

What struck me almost immediately was that every passage illustrated Taqwa. I whispered as much to Peggy as we sat down to listen to the homily. Or rather as she sat down to listen to it, because I was composing my own homily while the real one was in progress.

I never bothered to jot the homily down afterwards, but I remember some of its steps. One was a fleshing out of each of Jesus' images of watchfulness. In Luke 12:32–48 Jesus gives us, besides the image of the servants awaiting their master's return from his wedding, images of a householder sitting up to catch a thief and of two estate managers, one prudent, the other imprudent, responding to their master's delayed return in very different ways. The prudent one will act in the master's absence exactly as he would have acted if the master had been present.

So when the master does return, the prudent manager will be "put . . . in charge of all his possessions." The imprudent one, violently abusing his privilege, will "receive a severe beating" when the master returns.

I couldn't resist adding my favorite Gospel image of watchfulness, the parable of the ten virgins from Matthew 25:1–13:

Then the kingdom of heaven will be like this. Ten bridesmaids [translating the Greek word traditionally rendered "virgins" in a sense better suited to the context] took their lamps and went to meet the bridegroom. Five of them were foolish, and five were wise. When the foolish took their lamps, they took no oil with them; but the wise took flasks of oil with their lamps. As the bridegroom was delayed, all of them became drowsy and slept. But at midnight there was a shout, "Look! Here is the bridegroom! Come out to meet him!" Then all those bridesmaids got up and trimmed their lamps. The foolish said to the wise, "Give us some of your oil, for our lamps are going out." But the wise replied, "No! There will not be enough for you and for us; you had better go to the dealers and buy some for yourselves." And while they went to buy it, the bridegroom came, and those who were ready went with him into the wedding banquet; and the door was shut. Later the other bridesmaids came also, saying, "Lord, lord, open to us." But he replied, "Truly I tell you, I do not know you." Keep awake therefore, for you know neither the day nor the hour.

The thematic link between Taqwa and the ten virgins, as well as between the images of watchfulness in Luke (not to mention other images in Matthew, and in Mark too), is that both have to do with being awake and watchful for the signs of God's imminent arrival—or of our own imminent arrival before him.

Of course, there is a great thematic discontinuity as well, a discontinuity that the Christian-Muslim discussion still continues to flounder on: the gulf between Christian and Muslim claims about the identity of Jesus (to be discussed in a later chapter).

We don't have to be frightened by this and other discontinuities, however, or pretend they don't exist. We can look instead with hopeful confidence for the light that Salat and Taqwa throws on the ten virgins and on us too as we strive to live the Christian life more fully.

One question revealed by this light is why we Christians don't hear more about the ten virgins (and of the other images of watchfulness). Alertness to God's presence doesn't seem to be as important to us Christians as it is to Muslims. Monastic communities and contemplative prayer groups where mindfulness is practiced are exceptions. Perhaps most other Christians' weaker sense of the importance of alertness results from Christianity's gradual diluting or discarding of the eschatological perspective. Being awake used to be a key virtue, as Paul's first letter to the Thessalonians testifies, when Christians expected Jesus' return at any moment. But as this expectation was delayed, being awake ebbed in importance. We could say that other virtues, ones that had more to do with living in a prolonged between time, came in to replace it.

If this is so, we ought to be asking what we have lost by allowing the ten virgins to process to the wedding banquet without us. We join up with them (or with other images of watchfulness) only intermittently, when the Common Lectionary provides for them. Are we risking becoming identified with the five who are caught without oil in their flasks when the bridegroom comes?

The experience of Salat as a key means of reinforcing and ingraining Taqwa raises related questions. One has to do with what I call Christian sujud, the physical postures of our own prayer tradition. Returning to my Christian worship from Salat makes me wonder how mindfully we assume these postures, about whether they dispose us for God's grace as clearly and as vigorously as Muslim sujud disposes Muslims.

And more broadly: While it's true that in recent years many Christians outside monastic communities have been rediscovering not only contemplative prayer but the daily ritualized prayer forms that shape and sustain community, these changes need to go deeper, so that Christianity as a whole becomes marked by their fruits. Chief among them would be love of the neighbor, and of the enemy.

Forming such a critique isn't being negative about our Christian faith, as if the only purpose of studying another religion is to find fault with our own once we return. Nor is it to put the other religion, or in this case Islam, on a pedestal. It's to say, rather, that by meeting another religion we hope to become more faithful to our own baptismal promises. Sometimes that hope needs the stimulus of a self-critique born out of comparisons between ours and the other faith. Yet it is just as likely that hope will be stimulated in the opposite way—for example, by our understanding better what the other faith lacks or at least seems to undervalue.

The self-critique, when appropriate, works on two levels—the public level of church structures and tradition, and on the private level. To refer to my own case, for example, passing over into Salat and Taqwa and returning to the ten virgins forces me to examine with renewed urgency the amount of oil in my own lamp of faith—or the condition of my own "torch" of Taqwa. How much light am I actually spreading? How alert am I to the coming of the Bridegroom? If I'm as alert as I'd like to say I am, then why don't I live my Christian life more mindfully than I do? Daydreaming during Mass or composing my own self-pleasing homilies while the real one is in progress might seem like minor offenses. But what about my impatiences, my fretfulnesses, my dismissive judgments of those who don't share my opinions, my obsessions with whatever project I've identified as important and necessary? What happens to the torch of Taqwa when my own immediate concerns dominate my heart and imagination? How likely am I then to be living as if I could be standing before the Bridegroom at any moment, either to be invited into the party or to be shut out in the darkness forever? Why *don't* I pray for the gift of watchfulness and the psychological and spiritual poise that goes with it? Why *don't* I aspire to keep pace with the five wise virgins?

Of course, Muslims can and do stumble and lose their path in very similar ways. Having a strong commitment to the practice of Salat doesn't guarantee that the spirit will follow the letter. No concept or practice guarantees purity of niyya or intention. But at least Muslims have placed the problem of heedlessness front and center, along with very effective means of dealing with it.

I feel that many of my Muslim friends have more in common with the five wise virgins than I do, because the virtue of "keeping awake" is more deeply engrained in them than it is in me. But then I haven't credited to myself the benefit of the painful attempt to do sujud or bowing down to the ground. My aching knees remind me what I've gained from a tradition that puts keeping awake at its moral center. Sorely chastened by the experience, I can do the exercises necessary to bring action and intention together. Maybe, just maybe, I'll actually be able to join those five wise virgins in their procession to the bridal chamber. I, like them, might be able to enter the banquet and meet the Bridegroom, thanks to my watchfulness for the Bridegroom's arrival and to the right behavior that that arrival demands of me—the behavior that becomes the oil in my lamp.

As a Christian, I call this watchfulness the gift of the Holy Spirit. But from the perspective granted me by my attempt at sujud, I call it also the torch of Taqwa.

FOUR 'Abd and Wali, Martha and Mary

◆ Noises from the Back Seat ◆

I wasn't alone in the car. Dr. Shafiq was sitting beside me on the passenger seat. Ibrahim, an active member of the Islamic Center, was sitting in the back. I was driving my two friends down to visit the Trappist Abbey of the Genesee, in Piffard, New York.

I was still surprised that, in a previous conversation with Dr. Shafiq and Ibrahim about monasteries and about this particular monastery, which continues to be such an important witness to Peggy and me of contemplative Christian prayer—I was still surprised that Dr. Shafiq and Ibrahim had been so eager to visit the place. Why on earth would Muslims be interested in Christian monasteries? But I had yielded to what seemed to me Dr. Shafiq's and Ibrahim's caprice and agreed to drive them down, perhaps meet the abbot, and attend one of the Hours of prayer with the whole community.

It was a fine spring day. I became absorbed in my conversation with Dr. Shafiq and didn't pay particular attention to the fact that Ibrahim, usually very talkative, was not taking part in our exchange. Maybe he just wanted to enjoy fine views of the beautiful, burgeoning Genesee valley passing by outside his window.

Dr. Shafiq was displaying what I thought was an amazing knowledge of what monasteries were and what went on there. He knew a lot more than many Christians did. I asked him how he knew so much. Wasn't I familiar, he replied, with the passages in the Qur'an that talk about monks? No, I said, I wasn't.

"Allah praises monks," Dr. Shafiq explained. "But he doesn't want us to follow their example too far."

After I'd gotten home I looked up the references Dr. Shafiq then gave me. I found the passage that expresses God's praise in *sura al-ma'idah* 5:82-3:

. . . You will find that nearest in love to Muslim believers among non-believers are those who say, "We are Christians"—because among them are men who are devoted to learning [i.e., priests] as well as those who have fled from the world in fear [i.e., monks], for these never puff themselves up. And when they listen to the message of the Qur'an handed down to the messenger Muhammad, you see their eyes overflowing with tears. For they perceive at once its truth, and they pray, "O Lord, we believe—write us down among the witnesses. . . ."

The monks' fear is viewed positively because it accords with an Islam or self-yielding to God which vigorously rejects all competing idolatrous claims and worldly motives. In addition, the fear induces in them an openness to God's voice in the Qur'an. The voice penetrates their hearts. The tears that then fill their eyes express what Christians used to call compunction or penthos: sorrow for sin mixed with the hope of pardon. The monastic discipline of prayer cultivates this attitude.

But the monks' "fear" receives a negative evaluation in *sura al-hadid* 57:27:

> . . . We placed in the hearts of those who followed Jesus' compassion and mercy, but fleeing the world in fear [i.e., monasticism] which they brought forth as a novelty we did not prescribe for them. What we did prescribe was only to seek God's favor. They did not handle that command rightly.

In other words while the monks did well to flee the world, they fled too far. "Fear," according to the Qur'an, shouldn't lead to perpetual flight. Isolation and celibacy are selfish. Monks deny all interest in furthering the good of the ummah through the normal means of marrying, having families, and observing civic responsibilities. The Qur'an insists on keeping extremes in balance. Monks, for all of their signs of true islam, violate that balance, and so their excesses are held up as a warning.

These were details I had to look up for myself later on. I would have asked Dr. Shafiq to elaborate right then and there, but as we drove along I was becoming more and more distracted by a clicking sound coming from the back of the car. My imagination started to play tricks on me. Possibilities of disaster began to swirl and take form. Wheel bearing? Transmission? Hundreds of dollars for repair? Or—oh my God!—a sudden crunch and thud, loss of control, a swerve along the highway into opposing traffic? *Two Prominent Local Muslims Perish in Car Driven by Christian?*

I finally mentioned the clicking and my worry about it to Dr. Shafiq and Ibrahim. Had they heard it too?

The clicking stopped. There was silence in the car for a second. Out of the corner of my eye I could see Dr. Shafiq staring at me. Then both of them laughed. Dr. Shafiq said, "Oh, that's just Ibrahim's *dhikr*. He'll show you when we stop to buy something to take to our hosts."

At the supermarket, where a little later we picked up a gift basket of fruit, Ibrahim pulled a silver contraption from his pocket and displayed it to me proudly. "I just got this from Saudi Arabia. See? I press this button here each time I repeat *'La ilaha illa Allah'* ['There is no god but God'] and it counts them. I could do the same thing with a *tasbiyah*—a string of ninety-nine beads. What do you call it in English? Rosary? Thank you. This gadget is new, and, well . . . I like it better than beads!" He grinned.

I could never share Ibrahim's enthusiasm for the Saudi clicker, but I did want to know more about the prayer itself. What exactly was *dhikr*?

"Dhikr is remembrance," Ibrahim said, as we walked back to the car. "Remembrance of God that you try to make a part of your whole being. You choose one of the ninety-nine names of God from the Qur'an and you say it over and over till it becomes a part of you and everything else drops away."

I immediately thought of the Jesus Prayer and other techniques of entering into contemplation as practiced by the monks at the Abbey of the Genesee where we were heading. Maybe it wasn't so odd after all that Dr. Shafiq and Ibrahim had been so eager to make this trip. The Qur'an itself spoke of monasticism warmly if also critically. But besides that, the gap I'd assumed to exist between Islam and contemplative prayer—the prayer of the heart—seemed no gap at all. If Islam was a religion focused on orthopraxy, that is, on the correct performance of religious obligations, it was focused on an inner dimension as well. I'd simply been oblivious to its inner dimension till now.

Yet I wasn't just having second thoughts about Islam. I was having them also about Ibrahim himself.

If I'd been asked at that time to do a sketch of him, I'd have pointed to him as one of the Islamic Center's most knowledgeable and public figures. Whenever Dr. Shafiq returned to Pakistan for visits that sometimes became extended, Ibrahim was appointed the imam or leader in his place. In that role, he had to lead Salat, give the Friday *kutbah* or sermon to the whole gathered community, deal with the innumerable pastoral emergencies that came up each day, report to the Islamic Center's board, represent Islam publicly on committees and at functions. He'd once come to the school where I taught to give the benediction at graduation. And these don't by any means exhaust the imam's responsibilities. How did the private practice of dhikr fit in with such an active, extroverted life? How could an imam have time to get hold of a Saudi prayer-clicker, let alone actually use it? Why should he even bother? Where in Islam did it say that he was obliged to? Yet as I listened to Ibrahim give his explanation of dhikr, I couldn't help noticing how serene and fulfilled he looked. What felt to me like a confusion of role or maybe an oddity or eccentricity on his part clearly didn't feel that way to him.

On later occasions, as I delved deeper into the matter, I saw that more was involved here than feelings. Or rather, that Ibrahim's understanding of himself as public-spirited imam and as practitioner of dhikr was grounded on a basic duality within Islam itself, the duality expressed by the pairing of two dimensions of the Muslim personality. These dimensions are usually identified as 'Abd and Wali. The Muslim in his or her outer, active, extroverted dimension—that's the 'Abd. The Muslim in his or her inner, contemplative, introverted dimension—that's the Wali. But since in Islam all dualities are expressive of an even more fundamental unity, the 'Abd and the Wali don't represent separate roles or tendencies, but two sides of the same coin. Neither one can function without the other. They reach their respective perfection only when in balance with each other.

That the word 'Abd should represent Islam's extroverted, active face makes sense given the word's meaning: servant. The servant is devoted to fulfilling not his or her own private desires, but the true needs of others.

Those needs and the desire to serve them proceed from each person's islam. The Muslim becomes by necessity the 'Abd of the one to whom he or she has yielded—a servant of God. The consequence of the self-yielding is not the extinguishing of the 'Abd's will. The consequence is its perfection. The 'Abd now "must" do only those things which lead to his or her own flourishing. Yet what leads to his or her own flourishing is also what leads to the flourishing of every other 'Abd in the ummah. The personal and communal motive is perfectly blended.

This is the background against which the famous Five Pillars of Islam must be viewed. The Five Pillars lay down in schematic form the 'Abd's moral to-do list, the functions the 'Abd must perform to fulfill the terms of his or her Islam.

The first function is the performance of the Shahadah or Witness. It is very simple, yet all else depends on it. Shahadah consists in confessing before the members of the ummah, "There is no God but God, and Muhammad is his messenger." And that's all! No elaborate formula like the Nicene Creed—

just a declaration of the 'Abd's total life-allegiance along two planes. First along a vertical plane, the 'Abd pledges him or herself totally and exclusively to God. Then horizontally, the 'Abd declares his or her fidelity to Muhammad as the bearer of God's word in the Qur'an. By declaring allegiance to God and Muhammad at the same time, the 'Abd is not saying that the two are equal. The Qur'an insists that Muhammad was only a man. The 'Abd is saying that Muhammad deserves absolute trust. Muhammad alone mediates God's word faithfully.

The Shahadah is performed only once in the 'Abd's lifetime and is not so much an action in itself as a public commitment to the four specific actions that flow from it.

The first and most important of these is Salat, the cycle of five compulsory daily public prayers already discussed in Chapter Three. This first action is the most important because by it the 'Abd's Islam is most perfectly realized.

The second Pillar of the four remaining is Zakat or the purification of wealth. This is a fixed sum of income contributed each year to the poor. Zakat enjoins a redistribution of material resources from the haves to the have-nots. It also forces the haves to consider their original motives in acquiring wealth. Zakat tries to waken them from their illusion that the wealth they've accumulated is somehow inherently theirs rather than God's.

Next comes the yearly discipline of Sawm or fasting, especially during Ramadan. We'll talk about this Pillar in Chapter Six.

Finally, Hajj, the annual pilgrimage to Mecca to be performed once in a lifetime by those Muslims who are able and can afford to make the journey. More on Hajj in Chapter Seven.

The 'Abd is perfected by the sincerity with which he or she fulfills these requirements of the Shahadah. But how is the sincerity itself tested and perfected? The Five Pillars prescribe actions, but as Muslims themselves recognize, niyya or intention is everything. Fair-seeming actions may disguise impure motives. The Qur'an, like Jesus in the Gospels, weighs in with particular fierceness against hypocrisy. What is our guarantee that niyya and the action are one?

The Wali is that guarantor. The word *Wali* itself means friend or benefactor and even—depending on the context—saint. Representing the Muslim's contemplative side, Wali expresses interiority but not privacy. The Wali focuses on God and God alone. But this focus is not escapist or selfish. Far from it! The Wali's aim is the self's annihilation in God followed by its reconstitution. Purged of egoism, the self can be more purely dedicated to the service of others. The Wali at that point merges back into the 'Abd now healed of double motives and reinvigorated.

On a later occasion Ibrahim gave me an idea about how the Wali goes about this task of purification. He did so by responding to my request that he go into more detail about dhikr, the prayer he was practicing in the back seat of my car.

"Well," he said, "let's take as an example repeating the name of God, Allah. Everything depends on understanding how the doubled consonant works in Arabic as opposed to English. You know what I mean, don't you?" I nodded. Ibrahim was referring to the fact that in English, doubled consonants affect a pre-ceding vowel by shortening it, but they aren't themselves pronounced. If I pronounce the word "battle," for example, I say "ba" (short "a" instead of long "a") because of the doubled "t." But then I say "ttle," without putting any special stress or emphasis on the doubled "t." But if I were pronouncing "battle" in Arabic fashion, I would not only shorten the "a" vowel, I would pronounce the first syllable as "bat." Only then, without a break, would I add "tle." The sound resulting would be affected by the tongue's pressure on the front teeth to pronounce the double "tt."

That's what happens with "Allah." The word is not pronounced (as Westerners tend to do): A-llah, with stress on the "a" and with an unstressed, single "l." It is pronounced "All-ah." The tongue this time presses the upper palate, to blend both "l" sounds, before releasing the breath in the final syllable: "ah."

Why was Ibrahim making this point about doubled consonants? Because, pronounced correctly, the name "Allah" becomes a mantra of great power. You coordinate the intoning of Allah with your breathing. Breathe in slowly: "All-," allowing the body to feel the inner tension of the reverberating, doubled "l." Exhale: "ah," allowing the body to feel the release of breath as a sigh of delight and gratitude. Repeat this exercise ninety-nine times, moving through your beads—or clicking your fancy Saudi prayer-counter. Then do it again. Do it constantly. Never stop doing it! This was what you were made to do!

"Because you see," said Ibrahim, "what makes us human beings different from all other creatures is that God has breathed into us his *ar-ruh al-qudus* or holy spirit." Chanting the name Allah is the most powerful way given to us of expressing our gratitude for God's gift of ruh or spirit. We receive ruh, as it were, in the expansion of our lungs and we acknowledge the gift in our lungs' contraction, accompanied and fortified by the measured beating of our hearts.

Ibrahim then went on to talk about the physical benefits of the practice of dhikr. ("It goes right to the heart," he said. "It calms and heals the heart.") But what he really wanted to stress was the value of dhikr or remembrance itself—the remembrance of Allah, of course. Remembrance is such a key concept in Islam that one of the names the Qur'an uses of itself is *Al-Dhikr* or "the Remembrance." The importance results from the Qur'an's analysis of what blocks human beings from God—what hinders their loving intercourse with their Creator. We Christians name this interference sin: a self-administered corruption of our nature from which we are powerless to rescue ourselves except through grace. For Islam (which does not share the Christian concept of a "fall") the problem isn't sin but heedlessness, lethargy, willful self-absorption, proud obstinacy. We refuse to honor our primordial response to God's alastu or "Am I not your Lord?" The Qur'an tries to break through our carapace of indifference and self-sufficiency to bring us back to our senses. This is what it means to name the Qur'an *Al-Dhikr*, a phrase that might be better translated "The Wake-Up Call."

Both the 'Abd and the Wali hear this call, though they would not hear it with the same intonation. The 'Abd hears his or her dhikr or remembrance as a universal call to righteous external actions such as those that fulfill the demands of the Five Pillars. So the names of God among the ninety-nine that the 'Abd would remember with special energy and appreciation might be *Malik* or King and *Hakkim* or Judge. By contrast, the Wali hears his or her dhikr as a call to contemplative practices much like those used by Christian monks. The Name of God the Wali would remember might be *Wadud* or the Loving—or *Wali* itself, the Friend of friends.

Yet while each represents a separate, indispensable aspect of what is meant by dhikr, the 'Abd and Wali together represent a higher synthesis of opposites. As such, the unity of the 'Abd and Wali demonstrates Islam's essential nature as an ummah not only in balance itself but also called to mediate that balance to others:

> We have, in this way by giving the ummah a qiblah or direction for prayer, made of you a middle, justly balanced ummah that you might serve as witnesses or adjudicators over other peoples and that the messenger Muhammad might serve in the same role over you. (*sura al-bakarah* 2:143)

The 'Abd and Wali are inseparably bound together within each Muslim and within the ummah itself, and are an ayah or sign of such binding to humankind.

◆ Of Lawyers and Sufis ◆

OK, that's the ideal. But what's the reality?

Historically, here is what has happened: Islam has struggled to maintain the balance, achieving a high degree of balance during its finest hours (to pick two: in Baghdad during the Abbasid caliphate of Harun al-Rashid, 786–809 CE, and during the Moorish rule of Andalusia in Spain, 912–1085 CE), nearly losing its balance during the worst times (a downslide brought about in part by colonization of Muslim lands by the West beginning at the end of the eighteenth century and continuing very painfully into our own time).

A judgment like this doesn't mean there is something inherently "wrong" with Islam. The judgment merely says that any religion has a hard time living up to its ideals. We Christians have only to consider Christ's commandment that we "love your enemy" to realize how far short of the mark we ourselves have fallen, as individuals and as a community.

During the Hajj of 632 CE, when the people gathered on a mountaintop near Mecca to hear prophet Muhammad's Farewell Address, they were united as they were never to be again. The bloody rivalries and Bedouin vendettas of pre-Qur'anic days had been transformed by a religion which insisted that all humankind was united under one God. Time stood still, or as the prophet put it during his speech, "time has truly come full turn, to how it was the day Allah created the heavens and the earth."

Those who have gone on Hajj since then seek to reenter the mood of that occasion. They hear speakers from that same mountaintop exhorting them to moderation, as did Muhammad in the Farewell Address. They remember how their ancestors responded when the prophet repeatedly asked them, "Have I given the message?" And their ancestors said, with one voice, "O God, Yes!"

But inevitably the Hajj comes to an end. Muhammad must leave the mountain. The clock begins to turn again.

In 632 CE, Muhammad descended the mountain and a short while afterward died. A battle for succession immediately took place. The dispute pitted those who insisted that his successors should be democratically chosen from among the leaders of the now-united tribes, against those who insisted with equal vehemence that the succession should go to Muhammad's heirs. The dispute was settled violently. After the deaths of the first three successors, all drawn from the tribal leadership, Ali, Muhammad's younger cousin and husband of his daughter Fatima, was chosen as head of the ummah, thus seeming to vindicate the principle of family succession. But civil war ensued, and in 661 CE Ali was murdered by a member of an extremist faction that had formerly backed him. Power passed back to a member of the previous caliph's tribe, the Umayyads. Meanwhile the followers of Ali, calling themselves the *shiah-i-Ali* or "The Party of Ali," acclaimed Ali's second son and Muhammad's grandson Husain, as their caliph or leader. But Husain, marching against the Umayyads, was killed in battle on the plains of Kerbola by Yazid I, the Umayyad caliph. With this tragic stroke, the tribal principle seemed to have triumphed once for all.

Those who followed the family principle did not disappear, however. The Shi'a of Ali persisted as a semi-clandestine sect within the greater ummah. Their understanding of Islam, greatly affected by their political defeat and suppression, took on a mystical tone. Muhammad's own heirs were his true successors, they said, because only they possessed the true understanding of Islam hidden from the others. Their claim would be vindicated on Judgment Day when the last of those successors or imams would reappear to usher in the end of things. The invisibility or at least the marginality of an individual Shi'i (or member of the Party of Ali) would receive spiritual compensation in his or her present life by possession of the secret wisdom of succession, and political vindication in the future by the triumph of the family principle in the reemergence of the last imam and heir of the prophet.

In the terms of the 'Abd and Wali distinction we could say that the assassination of Ali created a tragic imbalance. Those belonging to Ali's party could not realize their identity as 'Abd. Sectarians, they could not function fully as members of the larger community, now called Sunni or followers of the Sunnah. Their energies flowed instead into the development of the Wali. Accordingly, a great part of Islamic spiritual writing derives from the Shi'i impulse to see in the Qur'an and in the *hadith* or sayings of prophet Muhammad secret references to the rightness of their cause.

A similar imbalance began to occur almost simultaneously among the Sunnis, but for a different reason. Muhammad was an Arab and envisioned the ummah as a perfected tribal unit. The gathering to whom he delivered his Farewell Address could not have numbered more than several thousands. They were people whose language he spoke and whose cultural values he understood very well.

If somehow time could have stood still for him and him alone and he had been able to stand on that same hill to address the Hajj gathering of 732 CE, the situation would have been very different. He would have looked out on a far bigger and more diverse ummah. By then, the small, tribal Arab Muslim community had spread out as far as Syria to the north, Spain to the west, and the Oxus River in India to the east. Some, at least, of the new converts present would not have known Arabic. Some would not have shared or understood Arabic tribal culture.

Islam too was influenced by the wider cultural contact. The tribal principle itself began to be shaken under the Umayyads, who moved the capital of Islam to Damascus and who began to treat the leadership of the ummah as their own dynastic right. It was altered almost beyond recognition when the Abbasid clan overthrew the Umayyads in 749 CE and moved the capital of Islam to Baghdad. Now began the era of Islam's world cultural dominance. But the model for command was no longer that of the Arabic tribal clan with a warrior chief at the helm, the model perfected in Muhammad himself. It was that of a luxurious Persian court governed by a Sultan or potentate who reigned from atop a vast hierarchical and bureaucratic pyramid. Nothing in the Qur'an envisioned or condoned such a thing.

Crushed under the weight of its own success, Islam tried to find its soul again. Somewhere under the debris of empire lay the 'Abd and Wali. It was essential to resurrect them. But what would they look like in this new dispensation, when the Islamicate—historian Marshall Hodgson's term for the complex and powerful political culture that developed around and transformed the prophet's message—dominated a vast part of the planet?

Lawyers and Sufis were the gradual answer. The Five Pillars still stood firm as general guidelines for the 'Abd's behavior. But a body of law had to be developed to govern Muslims' lives under the conditions dictated by the Abbasid sultanate. Though ultimate power belonged to the Sultan, many areas of domestic life could and should be brought under the control of regulations closely tied to the Qur'an's letter and spirit. Yet in the light of changed circumstances the Qur'anic letter in particular had to be reinterpreted. The vast body of Muslim jurisprudence that grew up to carry out this function was called the Shari'ah, from an Arabic word meaning "path to the watering hole."

The Wali reemerged in reaction to the profligacies of the Sultan's court. Calling themselves *Sufis* (a word probably based on the Arabic word for the plain wool robes they wore), those gifted with spiritual insight began to claim as a tradition the legends and sayings of previous Muslim ascetics and to build on those legends with their own highly diverse works of poetry and spiritual guidance.

The Qur'an's words about a "middle community" were not forgotten. While throughout the Abbasid period there was competition and occasional bad feeling between lawyers and

Sufis, the need for balance prevailed. Some of the greatest Islamic jurists have been Sufis. Most famous is Jalalludin Rumi (1207–75), the founder of the Whirling Dervish Sufi order and Islam's greatest poet, the inimitable poet of the mystical love of God. More systematically, the monumental thinker al-Ghazzali (d. 1111) forged a synthesis between 'Abd and Wali tendencies. Al-Ghazzali sought to show, on the one hand, that the inward work of a Wali is essential for breathing life into an 'Abd's external praxis; and to show, on the other hand, that the social structures upheld by an 'Abd gave grounding to a Wali's individualism.

The full story of these and later developments can't be told here. But we should at least take a glance at the current situation of Islam through the eyes of the 'Abd and Wali.

What we see is not heartening.

If Islam suffered distortion under the pressure of political success in its earlier period, it is suffering far greater distortion today under the pressure of political failure, a failure that owes much to two hundred years of colonization by Western countries and to the current American "war on terror."

Under this combined pressure the 'Abd and the Wali have parted company almost completely. Saudi Arabia offers an example of this tragic split. The reactionary Wahhabist brand of Islam favored by the Saud family sought to purge Islam of what it saw as foreign and particularly Western adulterations and to return it to its presumably pristine state at the time of Muhammad. Accordingly, the rich traditions handed down by 'Abds and Walis alike through the previous centuries of the Islamicate were eradicated. The lawyers and their schools of jurisprudence were banned. Shrines erected at the tombs of Sufi saints were eradicated, and Sufi orders (groups who formed around a spiritual leader, called a *shaikh* or *pir*) were abolished. A new kind of 'Abd emerged, without a Wali counterpart: a harsh overseer of puritanical adherence to the letter of the Qur'an. This 'Abd has triumphed in Saudi Arabia, but only by doing violence to the ummah as a "middle community."

Yet despite all its shocks and setbacks—some self-inflicted, others instigated or exacerbated by Western imperialism—Islam still seeks to recover its treasured balance between 'Abd and Wali, between its obedience to its outward duties and its fidelity to inward renewal. Whether and when it will find this balance again depends upon many factors—but among them is our encouragement of the balance. We Christians right here in the United States have an important role to play in that process. Many Muslims who have immigrated to the United States say that here, because of our political freedom and freedom of worship, they can more faithfully practice Islam than in their own countries. We Christians have everything to gain, as citizens and as faithful followers of Christ, by meeting our Muslim sisters and brothers in peace and openness, since these are as much the signs of balance in Christianity as they are in Islam.

◆ Martha and Mary ◆

Now as they went on their way, he entered a certain village, where a woman named Martha welcomed him into her home. She had a sister named Mary, who sat at the Lord's feet and listened to what he was saying. But Martha was distracted by her many tasks; so she came to him and asked, "Lord, do you not care that my sister has left me to do all the work by myself? Tell her then to help me." But the Lord answered her, "Martha, Martha, you are worried and distracted by many things; there is need of only one thing. Mary has chosen the better part, which will not be taken away from her." (Lk. 10:38–42)

This well-known Gospel story takes on a different look when we see it through the eyes of an 'Abd and a Wali—or better yet, through the eyes of a Muslim who embodies both tendencies and keeps them in balance.

Jesus, such a Muslim might say, is restoring that balance to Martha. As an 'Abd, her outward service has become all-consuming, having meaning only in itself. Worry (that is, over-concern about the performance of her duties) results, and she resents her sister Mary, who has not succumbed to Martha's obsession.

Instead, Mary "has chosen the better part." She "sat at the Lord's feet and listened to what he was saying." In the singlemindedness of her devotion to God's word, she is the exemplary Wali.

But, says our imagined Muslim, the point of the story isn't that a Wali has it all over an 'Abd. The story reinforces the need for constant readjustment of the relationship between the 'Abd tendency and the Wali tendency both within the individual and the community: in this case, within Mary and Martha separately and then within Martha's home (which she shares with Mary and—if these are the same people referred to in the Gospel of John—with their brother Lazarus). And even beyond that, within the community outside the house itself, a community that includes Jesus as treasured guest.

Our Muslim interpreter teaches us to look at Martha and Mary as complex symbols. Martha does possess the Wali dimension, otherwise she would not have welcomed Jesus into her home in the first place. In her gesture of hospitality we see the receptive, self-emptying aspect of the Wali. Mary, for her part, possesses the 'Abd dimension. She does not passively allow Jesus to distract her from her duties, she is not simply swept up or overwhelmed by him. She "has chosen the better part." Sitting at Jesus' feet is an act of will and discipline: characteristics more readily associated with the 'Abd.

So in this sense—looking at the matter still from the Muslim perspective—the "better part" isn't the exclusive reward of the Wali. The "better part" is what we identified in an earlier chapter as Taqwa or attentiveness to God. When Taqwa is central, the balance of the tendencies follows. Lose Taqwa, and worry and resentment and worse things follow for the 'Abd. Though the story of Martha and Mary does not tell it, a Mary who has lost Taqwa suffers also. She floats adrift within her private sphere of piety, oblivious to the needs of others.

As Christians, we should be able to appreciate an analysis like that. We can look at the increased interest in spirituality among Christians during the past half-century or so as a sign of how our religious culture has sought to readjust its own balance between the 'Abd and the Wali tendencies. Monasteries like the Abbey of the Genesee have become centers of spiritual revival for lay Christians—and not just lay Catholic Christians, as the popularity of books by Kathleen Norris and others indicates. Contemplative prayer groups flourish in local churches, and retreat centers across the country offer programs designed to help Christians find the necessary balance between their public worship and direct service and their inward life in God.

Where we and the Muslim, through whose eyes we looked at Martha's and Mary's story, part company is not over the 'Abd and Wali tendencies themselves or the need to keep them in balance. Where we'd part company is over the role Jesus plays in the balancing.

The Muslim wouldn't object to the role Jesus plays in calling both sisters, and particularly Martha, to a balanced relationship with God. In itself, this is a very "Muslim" activity. And he'd be with us in saying that the "better part" has something to do with a teaching that Jesus is communicating or even exemplifying in his own behavior.

The issue for the Muslim would be that we Christians want to see more in the scene with Martha and Mary than that. Because we go on to insist that the "better part" also refers, and refers primarily, to Jesus himself. Jesus *is* the teaching. He *is* the balance between 'Abd and Wali. Mary sits at his feet, not so much in respect as in awe. Martha knows she should be sitting there too, but has forgotten it. That is the point of both sisters calling Jesus *Lord*. Jesus is not simply a wise family friend, or even a saint. He is Emmanuel, God-with-us.

In order to make sense of the scene in somewhat the same way we Christians do, our Muslim friend would have to extract Jesus from Martha's home and substitute the Qur'an. We and our Muslim friend could then agree that it takes more than wisdom or exemplary human behavior to rouse the 'Abd and Wali in us and to bring them and keep them in harmony. It takes God's revelation, graciously embodied in the Word of God.

FIVE *Muhammad*
and the Virgin Mary

◆ Meeting Muhammad ◆

I'm continually meeting Muhammad in my conversations with Muslims. I cannot hear Muslims talk about their faith for long without being struck by how close they feel to Muhammad. Every time the prophet's name is mentioned—and his name is mentioned often, even when Islam itself isn't the topic—the speaker's face will light up, and he or she will immediately add either the phrase *salli Allahu 'aleihi wa-sallam* (abbreviated SAW) or the English translation "peace and blessing upon him" (abbreviated PBUH). Yes, it's customary for my Muslim friends to follow their mention of the names of the prophets preceding Muhammad—like Abraham, Moses, and Jesus—with the same formula. But my friends' tone in those cases, while respectful, lacks the joyousness that the name Muhammad commands. Just saying Muhammad's name seems to bring Muslims to life.

I meet Muhammad in the reflection of Muslims' love for him; in the love evoked by his name. This love attracts, because it's never frantic or overwrought. It's the sort of love that makes you stand up straighter, feel and look healthier, speak with greater wisdom and charity, listen more attentively—a grounding kind of love. If you were feeling lost before, you now see your way forward. If you were discouraged, you now have greater hope. It's a love that makes an outsider like me look around and ask, *who is the shining spirit who provokes such a response?*

Yet the joy Muslims radiate when they pronounce the prophet's name isn't obtrusive. They don't call attention to their joy, as if they thought they deserved special credit for feeling it. If pressed to give a reason for their reaction to the prophet's name, they'd probably shrug and say, "Well, it just comes from obeying God. We're only doing what we're asked to do." What they'd be referring to is the following verse from the Qur'an:

God and the angels send blessings on the prophet. O you who have faith, send blessings on him too and salute him with the word of Peace. (*sura al-ahzab* 33:56)

Built into Muslims' relation to the prophet is the divine command to bless him as the one through whom the Qur'an was handed down. But built in also is the command to salute Muhammad as if he were their contemporary. How is Muslims' sharing with the prophet in a common time and space understood? Muhammad died a long time ago, in 632 CE. Is his name alone enough to keep him alive in Muslims' eyes and hearts? The Qur'an itself does not give much substance to his name. It is mentioned there only four times—many fewer than the name of Jesus, for example (more than ten times), or than Moses (more than forty). It is true that Muhammad is directly addressed in many verses without being named, and in a few verses certain of the prophet's spiritual experiences are validated. Yet these verses are elliptical—as is so much of the Qur'an—

giving little reason for the animating force his name clearly exerts upon my Muslim friends.

I got my first clue to the origin of this force from the Islamic Center's bulletins. I used to examine each one carefully when it came in the mail. I'd find a list of the daily prayer times, advertisements for Muslim businesses, notices of pot-luck dinners and speakers, occasional financial statements, advice columns or articles explaining an upcoming celebration—the usual stuff found in church bulletins everywhere. But besides these universal elements there would be printed hadith or stories based on Muhammad's statements or behavior. Sometimes the hadith would be printed alone. Sometimes they would be connected to a particular theme. Their variety bewildered me. Some hadith addressed what seemed to me very mundane concerns ranging from proper etiquette at the dinner table to bodily hygiene. Other hadith offered spiritual advice of a very high order. What was the link that bound together such widely different directives? How did Muslims understand this diversity?

Here are examples of the diversity from a recent bulletin. The theme chosen for this issue was "Foods of the Prophet (SAW)." Various foods are listed, like water, milk, grapes, pomegranates, honey, and figs. Each food is given Muhammad's appraisal based on a hadith report. Of water the prophet said: "It is the best drink in this world. When you are thirsty, drink it by sips and not gulps, for gulping produces sickness of the liver." Of grapes: "They purify the blood, provide vigor and health, strengthen the kidneys, and clear the bowels." The burden of the list was to remind Muslims of a particular diet conducive to good physical and moral health and of moderation in following it.

Then, at the bottom of the page, in a shaded box all by itself, was a *hadith qudsi* or Holy Hadith. (A Holy Hadith is a first-person saying from God as reported by Muhammad but not considered a part of the Qur'an.):

On the authority of Abu Hurairah, who said that the Messenger of God said: "Allah said: 'I am as my servant thinks I am. I am with him when he makes mention of me. If he makes mention of me to himself, I make mention of him to myself. And if he makes mention of me in an assembly, I make mention of him in an assembly even greater. And if he approaches me a hand's span, I approach him by an arm's length. And if he approaches me by one arm's length, I approach him by six. And if he approaches me walking, I approach him at a run.'" (Bukhari, Muslim, Tirmidhi, Ibn Majah)

I'll explain below about the chain-like "he said's" at the beginning of the hadith and the names in parentheses at the end. Let's concentrate first on the hadith's content. God himself speaks in this hadith. The "servant" is the 'Abd, the earnest worshiper, the Muslim punctilious about fulfilling the requirements for Salat—requirements laid down in detail in other hadith. But in this particular hadith qudsi, God speaks not about what he requires of his 'Abd or servant. God speaks instead about his own response. It is a response that mirrors the 'Abd's own—"I am as my servant thinks I am"—though far exceeding it. The hadith's main point is to emphasize God's overwhelming mercy. Secondarily it puts in his or her place any 'Abd or servant whose piety has perhaps become excessive. If anyone thinks his or her devotion to God extraordinary, look how much more devoted God is to you! You can't measure God's mercy by the effort you make to obtain it.

This is a wonderfully vivid spiritual teaching. But how exactly does it connect to the mundaneness of diet and personal hygiene—the subjects of other hadith? What light do all hadith, mundane or not, throw on the question of the transformative power Muhammad's name exerts on Muslims?

The answer goes back, as all questions about Islam do, to the Qur'an. We saw that the Qur'an commands all Muslims not only to bless but also to salute the prophet with peace. But something else is required as well—emulation.

> For indeed you have in the messenger an excellent model to follow for the one who hopes in God and the Judgment Day and who remembers God constantly. (*sura al-ahzab* 33:21)

Muslims have taken this verse just as much to heart as the verse about blessing and saluting him. Even before the prophet's death they began to take minute notice of his every word, his every gesture. They weren't motivated by an idolizing impulse: The impulse was moral. It wasn't Muhammad himself they were seeking to emulate. It was the concrete realization in Muhammad's behavior of what it meant to be *amin* or faithful to the Qur'an. For this reason Muslims then and now refer to the prophet as the "living Qur'an." Muslim worship is incomplete if it is confined to a veneration of the Qur'an itself. Muslim worship reaches its fullness in emulation of the human being chosen by God to embody that worship at every moment of life, waking or sleeping, eating pomegranates or fasting, living at home or making defensive war. No human action ever performed by Muhammad, even the most private, and no pronouncement of his on any subject, however humble, is without value for

Muslim guidance. What is true for the prophet's humble pronouncements is true as well for his lofty ones, as in the hadith qudsi or Holy Hadith.

But how to bring to the ummah's attention the details of the prophet's speech and behavior? How to judge the accuracy of the flood of reports that began to come in, especially after the prophet's death? With time, memories of what the prophet actually said and did weakened. Memories were reshaped, twisted, even invented in order to advance a particular political position or outlook.

To sort authentic hadith or reports from inauthentic ones, a tradition of scholarship grew up in the first three centuries after the prophet's death. Scholars dedicated themselves to determining the quality of the *isnad* or "chain" of each hadith's oral transmission. The "he said . . ." form we saw at the beginning of the hadith qudsi above was employed to indicate the passing of the report from one speaker to another. If a scholar could show that a particular "chain" began with an actual close companion of the prophet and that the links on the isnad or chain—the people who transmitted the particular story from its original source—were trustworthy, then the scholar added the hadith to his collection. Certain scholars, like Bukhari and the other names listed at the end of the Holy Hadith above, were considered impeccable judges of hadith authenticity. Yet over the centuries, as the scholars' collections became unwieldy in size, special editions or digests had to be made so that the hadith could actually be accessible to Muslims eager to know whether their behavior in a certain situation followed the prophet's example or not. The whole point of the scholarship wasn't to produce an accurate biography: It was to produce a practical guide for living—in other words, sunnah or Way, Custom.

Taken merely as stories, without binding power on behavior, the hadith paint a portrait of Muhammad as a generous, open-hearted person completely dedicated to God and the building up of the ummah as a "middle, justly balanced community" (*sura al-bakarah* 2:143). The double thrust of Muhammad's advice in the hadith collections is toward moderation of behavior and the cultivation of salaam or peace in all situations. As an illustration, take the following hadith, picked from a popular modern hadith digest:

Hazrat Abu Zarr relates that the Holy Prophet (peace and blessing upon him) said: "Do not consider even the smallest good deed as insignificant. Even meeting your brother with a cheerful face is a good deed."[vi]

This hadith is typical in seeking to restrain the audience's passion for extremes or absolutes. Every minute of life is sacred, not just what we suppose to be its "peak" experiences. The sacredness of the moment is not honored privately, as measured by one's own state of pious fervor. The sacredness of the moment is honored in the healthy relationships that are brought about by disciplined attention to it. (We can see a comparable moderating effect in the hadith printed in the Islamic Center bulletin.)

Eventually, by the third Muslim century (tenth century CE), the hadith as sunnah, as practical guides to living, were organized into legal principles codified as shari'ah or law. Four great schools of Muslim fiqh or jurisprudence arose as a result. As complicated as Muslim law codes became, however, they all drew their power from a single source: from the ummah's belief that in Muhammad is found the purest form of human behavior before God. The previous prophets—including Jesus—exemplified it too. For various reasons the example in each of these cases was blurred, the pattern disturbed. By emulating Muhammad, Muslims are recovering the proper behavior of anyone who throughout the ages has said, "There is no God but God."

So the question about why the light goes on in Muslims' eyes when Muhammad's name is mentioned begins to answer itself. Muslims really do see Muhammad before them, in their own and in the behavior of their fellow Muslims, in so far as their behavior accords with sunnah. Muhammad is not God to them. There's no confusion between God and Muhammad for Muslims. But while Muhammad was born and died just like anyone else, he showed us more clearly than any other mortal what life is like when devoted to the ceaseless praise of God. Muslims are obliged to imitate that likeness. And so they do, in joy and gratitude.

◆ The Prophet's Life ◆

Muhammad was born around 570 CE into a minor clan of the tribe then dominant in Mecca, the *Quraish*. Mecca itself, like all inhabited areas in the Arabian peninsula, was little more than a collection of tents and stone dwellings around an oasis. The Meccan oasis was not a particularly fertile one. What distinguished Mecca was not its farms or sheep pastures but its location along an important trading route and its possession of the Ka'bah, the cultic shrine of the polytheistic Bedouin Arabs. The Quraish took advantage of those distinguishing features, and grew rich as camel merchants servicing the increasing trade between Syria and Palestine to the north and Yemen to the south and as hosts of the yearly Hajj. During

Hajj, Bedouin tribes from all over the peninsula, calling a truce to their interminable blood-feuding, would gather to pay respects to their particular deity among the 360 enshrined within the Ka'bah's walls. The Quraish collected sizeable rent from such visits.

Muhammad's life got off to a seemingly unlucky start. His father died before he was born, and his mother died when Muhammad was six. These losses threatened his very existence. Without family protection, no one survived for long, and orphans were more vulnerable than most. After his mother's death Muhammad found shelter with one of his grandfathers. But when his grandfather died before Muhammad had come of age, he was once again unprotected. Fortunately his uncle, Abu Talib, took Muhammad under his wing.

Muhammad's experiences of vulnerability give personal coloring to the Qur'an's adamant insistence that Muslims must take care of orphans and of all other marginalized groups like widows and beggars.

Muhammad's chief virtue as a youth wasn't boldness or athletic ability or martial zeal or poetic skill—virtues prized among Bedouins. Tradition also tells us that he was illiterate. His chief virtue was his sincerity and faithfulness. He was nicknamed *al-amin*, the faithful one. This virtue made him of little use as a warrior, but it did make him valuable within the new social group then emerging in Mecca, a settled, mercantile class dedicated to fostering the growing caravan trade. One member of this new class, a female entrepreneur by the name of Khadijah, a woman fifteen years Muhammad's senior, hired him because he was just the honest person she needed to manage her camel caravans. Muhammad's uprightness impressed her, as did his person. She proposed marriage, and he accepted. Disparity of age notwithstanding, their marriage was extremely strong and mutually supportive.

Polytheism was the dominant religion in Arabia at that time. As already mentioned, the Bedouins practiced it. But the peninsula also harbored groups of Christians and Jews as well as Zoroastrians along with other faiths hard to identify today. Muhammad was aware of these groups. During one of his caravan trips to the north during his youth, Muhammad had been identified by a Christian monk as the future prophet to the Arabs. We don't know what Muhammad thought about this pronouncement or about the religion he might at some point be prophesying. Yet we can assume that as he grew older he began to feel dissatisfaction with the polytheistic outlook with its emphasis on fate, its refusal to believe in life after death, its disdain for the poor, its narrow focus on individual glory and the good of one's own tribe and god to the exclusion of all others. A monotheistic outlook might have begun to appeal to him. What we do know for sure is that he began sometime before his fortieth year to retire regularly to a cave near Mecca in order to meditate. During one of these periods of meditation, in 610 CE, when Muhammad was forty years old, a revelation from God in the form of a qur'an or "reciting" of God's voice came down to him. Was he hearing the voice of a shaitan or devil? Was he mad? Khadijah resolved Muhammad's crisis of faith by persuading her husband that the revelation was truly sent by God. She won her husband over to belief in himself as God's prophet.

A year went by before he received another revelation. Two went by before Muhammad felt able to assume the responsibility of conveying what he had heard to the Meccans. From then on revelations came to him regularly throughout the twenty-two years of life remaining to him. These separate revelations or qur'ans or recitings were collected within a few decades after Muhammad's death in 632 CE. Together, they are known as the Qur'an, the Reciting par excellence.

The revelations which came down during the first twelve years, until the hijrah or emigration in 622 CE, directly attacked the Quraish's polytheism and its lack of moral restraint. Not surprisingly, Mecca became divided into two unequal but warring camps. Those who yielded themselves to the one God came mostly but not exclusively from disadvantaged groups like slaves, women, and marginal clan-members like Muhammad himself. Those who resisted the revelations tended to come from the leaders of the most powerful clans. They were the ones who had the most to lose. By embracing the Qur'an and Muhammad its messenger, the leaders would endanger the profitable Hajj trade. They would have to subscribe to a code of ethics that emphasized the good of the whole community rather than their own personal glory. They would have to reject their materialism and fatalism for what they regarded as Muhammad's absurd belief in life after death and final judgment.

The resistance of the clan leaders quickly grew into hostility. For a decade they were kept at bay by Abu Talib's protection of the prophet, though Muhammad's less-protected followers endured open persecution. Tensions mounted as Muhammad's preaching won more and more converts. Then things seemed to take a turn for the worse. Khadijah died in 620 CE, depriving the prophet of his chief moral supporter. A little later, when Abu Talib died, Muhammad found himself virtually defenseless. Attempts were made on his life. It looked as if the mission entrusted to him by God would fail.

It probably would have failed had not representatives of two Arab tribes from a town several hundred kilometers to the north called Yathrib arrived in Mecca. Impressed by Muhammad's moral character during previous visits to Mecca on Hajj, they now asked Muhammad to come to Yathrib with his followers (fewer than a hundred) to help the two tribes settle their disputes. Muhammad accepted the proposal, on condition that the tribes accept Islam. They did so, and returned to Yathrib. Muhammad sent out his followers in small groups so as not to attract the attention of the Quraish. Then in 622 CE he himself emigrated. This is the hijrah, year one on the Muslim calendar.

Islam, as we think of it, acquired its shape during the next ten years. During that short span of time, Muhammad was able to expand his tiny, persecuted straggle of followers into a unified ummah whose inner dynamic would, in the following century, transform the world. In achieving that expansion, Muhammad had to transform himself from the unremarkable though honest camel-merchant, and the persecuted prophet, into lawgiver, judge, army commander, and, finally, leader of all the Arab tribes. Islam grew from a religion directed primarily to questions of individual conversion and conscience to a religion laying out the basis for the harmonious coexistence not just of Arabs and Muslims but of the whole human family. Tiny, barren Mecca contained the seed of a mighty reformation in faith. Its central shrine, the Ka'bah, became the chief building block in the establishment of a just ummah or comprehensive human community.

But this expansion, while it might begin in Yathrib—later called *Medina al-nabi* or City of the Prophet—had to pass through Mecca. Even as Muhammad emigrated, he was determined that his mission in Mecca not fail. The hijrah would somehow provide him with the means to overcome the Quraish's hostility and to restore Mecca to its original focus as the site of monotheistic worship. The Ka'bah had been desecrated by the idols within it. Hadn't the Ka'bah been restored by Abraham and Ishmael from the remnants of Adam's original altar built for the worship of the one true God? Muhammad was determined to reclaim the Ka'bah for its true function. Only by doing so could the Arabs be persuaded that the revelations he had received were truly from God and binding upon them.

The remaining ten years of Muhammad's life were dedicated to this reclamation. Arriving in Yathrib/Medina, Muhammad successfully carried out the task of resolving the inter-tribal conflict that had brought him there. But Muhammad's goal was far wider than the settling of a particular dispute, and even wider than restoring Mecca to monotheism. He hoped to bring resolution to the wars and disputes within all humanity by bringing all people within the embrace of the ummah. His focus shifted and expanded under pressure of the revelations from God that he continued to receive but that now took a different direction. The revelations no longer addressed the situation of persecution in Mecca. They addressed the immediate challenges of building up an ummah of humankind beginning in Medina. The revelations from the Medina period therefore have a different character from the ones that came down to Muhammad in Mecca. The Medinan revelations tend to be prosaic, focusing on issues of governance and legislation instead of slicing like thunderbolts to awaken the sleeping conscience. These revelations answer hard questions about how unity can be brought to diverse human groups rather than focusing on the inner state of the individual listener.

Certain of these verses of the Qur'an have drawn criticism from non-Muslims. One kind of criticism focuses on Muhammad's nine marriages during the Medina period and the Qur'an's endorsement of them. Yet the Qur'anic endorsement is the last thing from a celebration of the prophet's libido. Polygamy was a fact of Arab life. But more important, the marriages themselves were a means of consolidating the ties binding the young ummah's many clans and tribes. They were also a way of dealing with serious questions of succession. Muhammad's two sons from Khadijah had both died in infancy. The eight other wives had a role to play in community-formation almost as important as Muhammad's own. The Qur'an names these women the "Mothers of the Believers" and enjoins on them particularly strict codes of behavior. We'll discuss one of those codes in the Hijab chapter.

Other Qur'anic verses drawing fire from non-Muslims are those that endorse the prophet's wars against Mecca. These were, however, defensive wars. The Meccans, alarmed by the ummah's growth, made war on Medina, attacking Medina twice. Both times Muhammad organized the town's defense. He led the men of the ummah in attacks against Meccan-owned camel caravans. It's important to remember that warlike behavior was the norm among Arab tribes at the time. What's unusual—and what reflects the true spirit of the salaam which the Qur'an sought to inculcate among the Arabs—is that when Mecca finally fell before Muhammad's army in 630 CE, the prophet did not slaughter the men and enslave the women and children, as would have been expected of him according to the Bedouin ethic. He entered the city without bloodshed. No Meccan was forced to convert to Islam.

Regardless of how Muhammad's means are judged, his end was always clearly in view and in great measure achieved. Beginning with the hijrah, Muhammad's goal was, first, the reclamation of Mecca for the one God and, second, the establishment of the ummah on a sound foundation. Islam is an experiment in practical human community, in life lived harmoniously among diverse populations thanks to a common vocation of praise of the one God. The praise itself does not have to take the form of Islam. All that is required is that each faith be true to its own founding principles. Islam itself never claimed to have invented those principles or to have discovered them for the first time. It claimed only to have recovered them from neglect and abuse. As the Qur'an many times reminded Muhammad, "You are only a warner." Muhammad's goal throughout the twenty-two years of his life as prophet of God was to be no more—nor no less—and to institute a community capable of keeping intact and transmitting that warning without dilution or addition in times to come.

◆ Muhammad and Mary, the Faithful Ones ◆

Shouldn't we be comparing Muhammad with Jesus instead? Yes—and no. Emphatically no.

Yes because as prophets Muhammad and Jesus set out on a similar path. Both of them emerged from obscurity—Jesus, the son of a carpenter, from an obscure Galilean peasant village; Muhammad, the camel merchant, from a fringe clan of the Quraish. Both received a heavenly mandate to preach God's word, calling for conversion and commitment to the building of a just community here on earth in the image of the kingdom of heaven.

But no, emphatically no, because Jesus was and is, for us Christians, far more than a prophet. Jesus' true identity as the

Word emerges by stages in the Gospel accounts. But Jesus' fundamental difference from Muhammad arises right at the beginning of Jesus' ministry. We know that Muhammad, at the beginning of his own ministry, is commissioned only to bear the qur'an, the reciting. He is not its source. By contrast, God's voice at Jesus' baptism, by naming Jesus as his Son (Lk. 3:22; Mt. 3:17; Mk. 1:11), implicitly commissions Jesus to speak on God's behalf—a connection made clear on the mountain of Transfiguration when God commands, "listen to him" (Lk. 9:35; Mt. 17:5; Mk. 9:7). Jesus' very person is the message. He *is* God's voice.

Jesus' revealed identity as Word is decisive in separating him from Muhammad. Because of that identity and of what follows from it in the Gospel story—Jesus' death and resurrection—Christians cannot equate Jesus and Muhammad. Interestingly, Muslims cannot equate them either—though for opposite reasons. We Christians cannot equate them because to do so diminishes Jesus' true identity as Word of God. Muslims cannot equate them because to do so turns Muhammad into an idol or deity rivaling God himself!

Of course, we would all be talking here about the Jesus of the New Testament. The Jesus of the Qur'an—renamed *'Isa*—is very much kin to Muhammad because he is Muhammad's immediate precursor in the ancient line of prophets ending in their "seal," Muhammad himself. We'll focus on the relation between the New Testament Jesus and the Qur'anic 'Isa in a later chapter. But for now, what we need is a way to return from Muhammad to our own faith. If the New Testament Jesus is not the bridging figure, who in our New Testament is?

Enter Mary.

Muslims love her. She is the only female identified by name in the Qur'an. Her name even appears as the title of one of the Qur'an's suras or chapters. She is spoken of in the Qur'an far more often than she is in the New Testament, and always in terms of the highest praise. In the Qur'an's version of the Annunciation, for example, the angels address Mary as follows:

> O Mary, indeed God has chosen you and has purified you, and has chosen you above the women of all the worlds. (*sura al-'imran* 3:42)

She has been chosen to bear God's *kalam* or word. She and she alone among all women is God's choice to be the vessel of the divine action producing a human being—without male intervention. This kalam or word of God will become a great prophet, Jesus, whom the Qur'an knows as 'Isa.

God selected both Muhammad and Mary as mere mortals, to be bearers of the word.

Ah, but caution is in order here.

First, there is an obvious difference, and a great one, between the Muslim and Christian understanding of "word." Even when the Qur'an uses kalam to refer to Jesus, it is not employing the term as John does in his Gospel, as the Logos or Word. Kalam is used metaphorically, pointing either to God's creative power or to Jesus' prophetic mission, a mission exactly like that of all previous prophets.

Second, just because she bears the kalam—as opposed to the Word or Logos—the Mary of the Qur'an is not identical with the Mary of the New Testament. Their natures differ depending on whether it is Jesus or 'Isa whom they carry in their wombs. And for all the honor due to the Qur'anic Mary for bearing the word in the form of the prophet 'Isa, Muhammad is due more because it was through him that the Qur'an itself—known as the *kalimat allah* or Word of God—came into the world.

But here is an interesting twist. We drew an analogy earlier between the Qur'an and the risen Christ's continuing presence among us in Scripture and sacrament. The analogy can be extended now to associate Muhammad and Mary (the New Testament Mary) as the primary bearers of both Words.

Muhammad's and Mary's qualification for their roles as bearers of the divine Word are similar as well. One such qualification is that both have been "purified"—a condition that the Qur'an, like the New Testament, expresses in terms of Mary's virginity. But the Qur'an expresses the purification also in terms of Muhammad's illiteracy. Both Muhammad and the Mary of both accounts "conceive" of the word in perfect union with the gracious will of God, no motive or power of their own coming between the divine will and their own. The Islam or self-yielding of both is perfect. This fact, in relation to Mary, is even more clearly expressed in relation to the New Testament Mary than in relation to the Qur'anic one. There is no passage in the Qur'an that corresponds to Mary's words of acceptance in the Gospel of Luke: "Here am I, the servant of the Lord; let it be with me according to your word." (Lk. 1:38) Mary's language and tone here are thoroughly Qur'anic—a cause for wonder and meditation for those of us who treasure these lines as a model of Christian faith commitment!

We now leave the Qur'anic Mary behind us, for it is with the Mary of the New Testament and with her alone that Muhammad shares at least three other key qualifications as bearer and exemplar of the divine Word.

Both demonstrate unwavering commitment to the prophetic call for social justice. We've already looked at the Qur'an's emphasis on solidarity with the poor and the marginalized as well as at Muhammad's own personal identification with orphans and outcasts. The same emphasis can be seen in Jesus' teachings, of course. But it can also be seen in Mary's exultant cry in her Magnificat, a cry amplified by her own experience as a marginalized person:

> His mercy is for those who fear him
> from generation to generation.
> He has shown strength with his arm;
> he has scattered the proud in the thoughts of their
> hearts.
> He has brought down the powerful from their thrones,
> and lifted up the lowly;
> he has filled the hungry with good things,
> and sent the rich away empty. (Lk. 1:50–53)

The content is Qur'anic, if the idiom is different.

Another qualification both shared is suggested by the first two. Muhammad and Mary are examples of the whole human being. The fact that they display qualities of total receptiveness on the one hand and prophetic boldness and vigor on the other, points not to a split in their personalities, but to integration. The perfection of human nature Muslims attribute to Muhammad means that in him we see imaged the original unity of the human personality, his inward, receptive qualities emerging in his Islam balanced by his active, extroverted qualities emerging in his prophetic vocation as it matured during the Medinan period. We sense a similar balance of receptive and active qualities in Mary, though we know far less about her. Her human perfection is expressed in Roman Catholic doctrine as the result of her Immaculate Conception. The fact that this balance appears in prophetic figures of opposite gender is itself a miracle, given the patriarchalism of the cultures in which both Muhammad and Mary lived.

What Muhammad and Mary have most in common is that they were trustworthy—*aminun*, faithful ones, the plural form of the nickname *al-amin* given to Muhammad. They devoted themselves wholly to the service of the word they carried, a devotion manifested in the exemplary behavior of both. Mary's behavior wasn't noted and remembered in anything like the detail that Muhammad's was, but from the glimpses we're given of her throughout the Gospels and in Acts, we get the picture of a faithfulness so graced that it carried her through the unimaginably bitter disaster of the crucifixion into the life of the new Church that formed around her Son's risen body. Mary's presence with the other disciples after Jesus' ascension (Acts 1:14) and almost certainly soon after at Pentecost is symmetrical with Muhammad's own return to Mecca in triumph. Both Muhammad and Mary lived to see the fulfillment of the Word to which they had yielded themselves.

Whatever their sufferings had been—and in Mary's case they were measureless—their joy was even greater. In the hope of sharing that joy with them, Muslims take Muhammad as their model and an increasing number of us Christians take Mary as ours. Maybe the day will come when each other's models can become our own as well.

SIX *Ramadan* and *Christmas* *(Lent and Easter Too!)*

◆ Ramadan as Both Feast and Fast ◆

Women in colorful outer garments and *hijabs* (or head scarves) bearing platters of delicious-smelling food, men greeting each other with smiles and hugs, children running at top speed, shrieking, getting in everyone's way—a bubbling up of energy transforming the narrow corridor of the Islamic Center into peaceful bedlam: my abrupt introduction to Ramadan.

Innocently unsuspecting, I had been sitting, before the people and the food arrived, at the back of the masjid with my Qur'an teacher, Omar. I had been sounding out some Qur'anic lines and fumbling through a translation of them while Omar listened, patiently correcting me. The winter dusk thickened outside. I grew sleepy, as did he. We stopped for the day. All was quiet. But by the time I had packed up my books and stretched my legs, getting some circulation back into them (Omar and I had been sitting cross-legged on the carpeted floor), there was already a buzz in the Center's entryway. It was the first time my Saturday appointment with Omar fell during the month of Ramadan, so I wasn't prepared for the hullabaloo. I'd heard about Ramadan, of course. Omar and I had already worked laboriously through the verses in *sura al-bakarah* or "The Heifer" in which God enjoins Ramadan on all believers, but I hadn't experienced the event for myself. *This is my trial by fire*, I thought, as the children erupting from every corner seemed about to sweep me away.

Omar laughed when he saw how alarmed I looked. "They're all hungry," he said. "Remember that we Muslims haven't eaten food or had anything to drink since before dawn. But now it's time to break our fast." Then he added, "You should join us sometime!"

I did so, on a later occasion, and on many occasions during Ramadans in subsequent years, usually accompanied by my wife. Most often, as I learned afterwards, the evening breaking of the fast would occur in smaller settings where just a few families and close friends would gather, first in one family's home, then in another's. The Islamic Center itself would host those without homes, or at least without homes in the area—Muslim students at Rochester's colleges and universities, for example. On weekends and on special occasions during Ramadan—when non-Muslim guests like us were invited, or when a renowned speaker came to town—the Rochester ummah would gather at the Center. On occasions like that, the cuisine would be the responsibility of a particular national immigrant group. Muslims from the Indian subcontinent would provide food different from that of African Muslims, for example. Then, at the end of Ramadan, the whole ummah would gather for the *eid-al fitr*, the feast breaking the fast for the last time, in thanksgiving for all God's mercies revealed during the month just ended.

There was never anything fussy or complicated about these gatherings. We would assemble in the Islamic Center's general meeting area upstairs. The platters of food would have made their way to the buffet tables. After a mercifully short prayer, we would be invited to partake. I tried not to seem to be in a rush as I walked up to the buffet, or to look too embarrassed when I would be (as always happened) invited to break into the already-long line. I hoped I didn't look too greedy as I sampled from every dish, even those that looked unfamiliar to me. Most of all, I tried not to feel guilty about the fact that I hadn't "earned" the right to be enjoying the meal so much— for in my own case no fast-breaking was involved. But my Muslim friends didn't seem to care whether I'd fasted or not. They were too busy gobbling up the good, home-cooked food to notice. So, carefully lowering my heavily laden paper plate to a place at one of the long tables set up in the conference area, I would immediately dig in. My wife would sometimes eat with me, sometimes with the women in the women's section, depending on the customs of the hosts that evening. But whatever the arrangements, we always felt a little awed by the hospitality which by now almost seemed to us synonymous with Islam.

The meal would often be followed by a speech by a visiting scholar or dignitary. I don't recall any of these eminent personages with their probably excellent messages now, alas. But I do have a memory of certain of my fellow guests during the Ramadan following September 11. In response to the American public's widespread fear of Muslims generated by the terrorist attacks, the Islamic Center had made a policy of inviting to a succession of Saturday Ramadan meals various groups of non-Muslims from the Rochester community: lawyers, business people, academics, etc. But the invitation that most impressed me was the one the Center made to its own neighbors—non-Muslims living in a housing development located nearby. Extravagant in their Ramadan dress and feasting, my Muslim friends were extravagant also in their courageous hospitality. For, sad to say, not every such invitation was welcomed. But those neighbors who came seemed to appreciate the food and hospitality as much as my wife and I did.

Of course there was and always must be a limit to non-Muslims' appreciation, because we non-Muslims haven't shared in the discipline of the fast that precedes and gives point and flavor to the banquet afterward. It's not just that the food must taste better when Muslims finally break a Ramadan fast: It's that they have undertaken the fast as a way of praising God with renewed attention, with renewed Taqwa. At the same time they have rededicated themselves to building up the ummah by means of the daily discipline and celebration. The praising and the rededicating are profoundly and concretely interrelated and communal. A Muslim who must break her Ramadan fast alone must feel keenly the deprivation of the family or community breaking the fast and giving thanks to God with her. Only in a community setting does the distinctive rhythm of Ramadan make sense: The daily pulse of fasting and celebration and praise moves like a wave with valley and peak throughout the month.

But there's another limit to our—that is, non-Muslims'—appreciation of Ramadan. We simply don't have a comparable experience in respect to fasting. Yes, we can compare Ramadan fasting with the fasting some Christian churches still practice in Lent. But if we do, we're likely to come away feeling chastened. We Christians talk about fasting as a key Lenten discipline, along with prayer and almsgiving, but our actual practice of fasting is meager indeed—limited to Ash Wednesday and Good Friday and the Lenten Fridays in between. Even then we fail to treat fasting as a communal discipline, as an activity we celebrate publicly. We certainly don't connect fasting with its release in nightly fast-breaking. Those two elements—the fasting and the feasting—which I said earlier seemed contradictory, are actually poles of a kind of communal flexing and relaxation of will, of inhalation and exhalation, of collective breath on the part of believers. Only from the outside do the two poles at first seem unrelated.

The fast from food during the daylight hours, as well as from drink and from all other discretionary satisfactions of appetite (including sexual ones), is the key part of Ramadan discipline, of course. But another important part is the discipline of Ramadan evening worship called *tarawih*. During a succession of these evenings, the ummah gathers to recite the Qur'an in its entirety. Recently I was invited to one such evening. By the time I arrived, the ummah had already gathered in the masjid to hear the *hafiz*, a qari or reciter who knows the Qur'an by heart, proclaim the Qur'an. The reciting is done over the length of the month of Ramadan. (The Qur'an is about the same length as the New Testament.) Before the hafiz begins, the men line up side by side as they do for Salat or the five daily prayers by facing the qiblah or the direction to Mecca. The women are doing the same in their balcony above. The hafiz starts at that part of the Qur'an where he left off the evening before, using breaking-off places marked in the text. He introduces each section by chanting the opening sura of the Qur'an. The men and women say "amen" at the prayer's conclusion, and then perform sujud or the prescribed cycle of bowing and standing not only before and after the reciting that ensues, but also between designated subsections. This cycle of repeated prayer and sujud and attentive listening while standing in line continues for the next hour and a half, until the designated section for that evening has been completed.

Sitting cross-legged at the back of the masjid as I normally did when studying with Omar, with my copy of the Qur'an propped on my knees—propped carefully, so that it touched neither my stocking feet nor the rug—I tried to find and follow the verses the hafiz was reciting. But I couldn't catch up to his rapid pace. Part of the problem was that the Qur'an, except for *sura Yusuf* and for short stretches in other suras, tends to be allusive rather than narrative. Without a story line to catch on to, I was lost. I felt frustrated, and wished I'd gotten oriented in the text before the hafiz began.

But my mood changed when at one point a man broke from the prayer-line, went to the shelf at a sidewall where copies of the Qur'an were available, and began to leaf through one of them. After a few minutes of searching, he approached me to ask if *I* knew the place! I shook my head no, in seeming regret, but secretly proud that I'd been asked—and at the same time amused at my surge of vanity. He sighed and rejoined the line.

I shut my copy of the Qur'an at last, stretched my legs, breathed deeply, and tried to set aside my own agenda for an appreciation of the human effort in progress all around me. There was no doubt that *tarawih* exacted a toll from each participant. I watched with sympathy as some of the men came in late and rushed to join the line that was now four deep. Others, obviously bound by worldly commitments, were forced to leave early. Then I noticed a little girl about four years old who clung to a man standing in the rear prayer line—obviously her dad. For a while she bravely tried to amuse herself, sometimes stretching the straps of her red jumper over her shoulders, sometimes imitating the movements of sujud. When she pulled at her dad's trousers from time to time to get his attention, he turned and gently asked her to be patient—I couldn't hear him say that, but as a father and now a grandfather myself, I could lip-read to perfection the universal language he was speaking to her in. When finally the little girl became weary and unhappy, her dad quietly led her away in the midst of the reciting. It was a scene between parent and child undoubtedly being repeated much more frequently in the women's balcony above.

But all such efforts by members of the community to make good on their commitment to tarawih, brave as those efforts were, paled beside the effort of the hafiz, of the one who knew the whole Qur'an by heart. More than a feat of memory was in question here. Yes, granted: a tremendous investment of time and mental energy was demanded of the would-be hafiz. I'd heard that the successful ones almost always have to begin the project as children, while their minds are still flexible and free from clutter. Of course, the mere words without an understanding, not simply of their meanings but of their provenance—from the mouth of God—would be dry shells. Still, not even understanding was enough. As the Qur'an says, "The trusted Spirit brought the revelation down upon your heart" (*sura al-shu'ara'* 26:194). To Muhammad's heart, not simply to his lips. The point is that the reciting of the Qur'an—the Qur'an as qur'an or recitation—transforms the person reciting, just as it transformed Muhammad himself from a successful Mecca merchant to the founder of a world religion. It does not transform by force, however. A famous verse of the Qur'an says, "Let there be no compulsion in religion" (*sura al-baqarah* 2:256). Yet even though the Qur'an came down whole from God, it did not come down as an alien element. It was somehow, while always and forever purely of God, always and forever intimately human. "We [i.e., God is speaking] are as close as your jugular vein," says another famous passage of the Qur'an (*sura qaf* 50:16).

So for the hafiz, I reflected, to know the Qur'an *by heart* (the idiom, "know by heart," is the same in Arabic as in English) was to know it *in his heart*. It wasn't just a case of the hafiz's giving major space in his memory to "the remembrance"—that is, to the Qur'an. It was even more a case of his attributing that remembrance to himself, to his own memory of himself. And by occupying that space, the Qur'an became a living presence within him.

Well . . . almost but not quite. No one is perfect. No mortal can fully embody God's voice or absorb it as his or her own. At a couple of points during the evening's recitings the hafiz clearly made a slip—either forgot or dropped a line. A man standing next to him to help out in such emergencies quietly corrected him. (This man held a copy of the Qur'an and had been following the text attentively.) The hafiz recited the missed or muffed line again and went on. God is merciful. Didn't God have to warn even Muhammad not to rush his reciting so as to anticipate words before God had actually sent them down? (*sura al-giyamah* 75:16) God doesn't want mechanical perfection, but Taqwa, attentiveness.

Ultimately the reward is a feast in the next life, near rivers of cool water. Ramadan celebration is the foretaste of that celebration to end all celebrations. Nerves can't be forever on the stretch. Even hafizes have to catch their breath. Even good little girls in red jumpers have to see their mothers and play and get something to eat once in a while. Ramadan alters the saying about feast and famine. Not either/or but both/and. Either feast or famine becomes feast *and* famine: the two beautifully adapted to the ebb and flow of human will and strength.

◆ Catching Muhammad's Gratitude ◆

Ramadan, with its movement between stress and relaxation, is, as we said earlier, a profoundly communal event. But it is rooted in a profoundly personal one, the handing down of the revelation of God to the prophet Muhammad. The handing down tested Muhammad to the limit. To be chosen to receive the divine word is not a cause for self-congratulation. The Hebrew prophets and Mary herself attest to this. There is joy, yes, but there is terror, or at least a profound bewilderment. There is an overwhelming desire to answer this call, as in the "Send me" of Isaiah. There can be an equally overwhelming desire to flee or to excuse oneself from it—Jonah comes to mind, and Jeremiah. But, whether one approaches or retreats, no safe distance, no control of the experience is possible. One is in the hands of God.

Various legends surround Muhammad's distress at being the recipient of God's word, especially during the initial burst of the revelation, during the *lailat qadr* or "night of power or destiny" now celebrated towards the end of the month of Ramadan. His first wife, Khadijah, plays a big role in these legends. We hear how she wrapped him in blankets or robes to warm him from the chill caused by the stress and the uncertainty. Muhammad kept asking himself: Is this revelation true? Or the voice of Satan? Khadijah is supposed to have assured him that what he had heard was indeed God's voice.

The specifics of Muhammad's reaction to that voice may be legendary, but what the voice itself said is not. That first revelatory burst now forms the initial five lines of *sura al-'alaq*, "The Clot of Blood" (or "embryo") 96:1-5:

Recite, in the name of your Lord, who
Created humankind out of a blood clot
Recite, for your Lord is most generous
Who taught by the word
Taught humankind what it did not know. . . .

Part of the power of this language comes from certain effects that can't be translated: the rhyming of Arabic words at the ends of lines 1 and 2, and of 3 through 5, for example. There is an ironical play with the words for "taught" and "did [not] know"—ironical because while these words come from the same Arabic root, they have such different meanings when applied to God and then to humankind. But three key assertions are clear enough in any translation. One assertion is that the revelation isn't for Muhammad's ears alone; it is to be proclaimed, to become public, or to be, literally "recited" (from the root *qar'a* meaning recite—qur'an is the root's noun form). A second assertion is that "your Lord" is all powerful. The God who can create humankind from a clot of blood can do whatever God wills. (In later suras, this assertion becomes the basis of God's claim to be able to raise the dead to life again; the same God who turned a clot of blood into a human being can raise up to new life a clod of dust.) The third assertion is that this same God is "most generous"—or more accurately, "beyond all comparison for generosity." All-powerful as God is, God is by the same infinite measure gracious, and is a God moreover who relates to us through reason (or "word"), seeking to influence us not by force but by teaching or persuasion.

This qur'an was a thunderclap, a "night of power" indeed, one that not only overturned at one stroke the polytheistic traditions in which Muhammad had been brought up, but that also commanded Muhammad himself, in the revelation's very first word, a verb in the imperative mood—"Recite!"—to play an extremely significant role in the overturning.

Perhaps God's mercy was nowhere better shown than by God's subsequent, though temporary, silence. Months, maybe a year, went by before Muhammad received a second revelation. As if God were giving Muhammad time to build his strength for further revelations and the trials they would occasion: trials resulting from the hostility to the revelations of his own Quraish tribesmen in Mecca.

There was then and still is cause for celebration as well. As real as the difficulties are, the rewards are greater. Those rewards aren't spelled out in that first sura, *ura al-'alaq*, but in a later one, *sura al-bakarah*, revealed in Medina, where Muhammad was finally able to assemble the Muslim ummah. In verses 185–188 of *sura al-bakarah*, God first makes clear that the purpose of Ramadan fasting and celebration is to "glorify God for his having sent down the Qur'an as your guidance." And God adds, in a phrase of divine irony that occurs often in the Qur'an, "so perhaps—who knows?—you may actually be grateful!" In any case, God does not intend the fast to be a burden on people, and so makes allowances for those who are ill or on a journey. They can make up the fast later, God says. And fasting should be understood in the widest sense. Not just the gobbling up of food is forbidden. But also the gobbling up of one's wealth, either gobbling it up oneself to satisfy one's own whims or to tease others into gobbling it up by dangling it before them—especially before judges, thus corrupting them.

As for the reward, what could be greater than intimacy with our creator? The Qur'an puts it this way:

When my servants ask you about me
Tell them I am very close
I answer the prayer of every pray-er
When he prays to me
But let them also answer to me
And believe in me
Perhaps—who knows?—they may walk in the right
  way. (*sura al-baqarah* 2:186)

The subtle play on words—on the word for "pray, prayer, pray-er" and on the word for "answer," used in one verbal form for people and in another for God—hints at a tenderness in God's relation to humankind that is a key feature of the Qur'an and a reason why gratitude has always been and continues to be the most appropriate human response to that tenderness.

Ramadan tries to capture the gratitude felt initially by Muhammad and then transmitted by means of the month-long celebration down the ages to all subsequent believers. As much as possible, Muslims try to participate in Muhammad's experience by focusing their attention through sawm or fasting, by devoting themselves, through the performance by the hafiz, and by the exercise of their Taqwa or attentiveness, to the absorption of the word—and by feasting afterward in anticipation of the heavenly banquet to which all whose hearts are pure will be called.

◆ Christmas, Lent, and Easter in the Light of Ramadan ◆

How does an immersion in Ramadan affect the way we see our own Christian celebrations? We discussed one of those changes earlier: the less than satisfactory judgment we find ourselves passing on Lenten fasting, a custom perhaps more honored in the breach than in the observance.

Yet the negative judgment should have a positive effect. It should stimulate us to reexamine our practice of fasting and to ask ourselves whether it could be done communally, in a disciplined and celebratory spirit. The point wouldn't be to imitate Ramadan fasting but to reinvigorate our own tradition. Many of the motives that inform Muslim fasting overlap with the motives of Christians fasting: control of merely fleshly desires, greater solidarity with the poor, stronger attention to God (along with a sharpened sense of what all too often weakens or distracts such attention). How could our communal fasting express better than it does now a Christian celebration of these disciplines?

Lent is only the most obvious of the Christian connections we can make from within our immersion in Ramadan. Ramadan also connects us with Christmas, with the crib in Bethlehem. In this area we cannot accuse ourselves of a failure to celebrate! Here we touch on a parallelism discussed in the previous chapter, between the incarnation of the Logos (Word) in Jesus of Nazareth and what is called the "inlibration" (literally, "embookment") of God's kalam or word in the recitation sent to Muhammad beginning during the "night of power." Along with Muslims at Ramadan, we Christians at Christmas celebrate God's gracious sharing of himself with us mortals, without insisting that our own understanding of how that sharing happens has to be brought in line with others'.

Yet Ramadan's perhaps most fruitful connection to our Christian practices is with Easter. We're noting here the respective moment of fullness of Muslim and Christian revelation. The "inlibration" of God's word in the "clear Arabic" of the Qur'an occurred during the "night of power." While the revelation of the whole Qur'an to *us* occurred over time—beginning on the "night of power" and ending with Muhammad's death twenty-two years later—the Qur'an did not in itself become more complete, more developed, over that period. By contrast, the full meaning of God's self-communication, as we Christians understand it, is revealed, not in the Incarnation itself, but in the Paschal Mystery. If we Christians have an event corresponding to a "night of power," it is here, between Good Friday and Easter dawn.

In one sense, of course, the comparison between Ramadan and Easter throws the strongest possible light on Muslim and Christian differences. Partly the difference has to do with our different conceptions of time: more retrospective than progressive for Muslims, more progressive than retrospective for Christians. The Qur'an calls us constantly to remembrance or dhikr. The Qur'an itself is sometimes referred to as al-Dhikr, the Remembrance. The Alastu—"Am I not your Lord?" spoken to us at our creation—roots us immovably in our age-old promise. By contrast, Christians are always called forward. "Follow me," Jesus says. We are on a journey into a future and to a city still under construction.

But the difference in our conceptions or evaluations of time flow from an even deeper difference: the difference in our understandings of God. It's not simply that there's no corresponding notion of the Paschal mystery in Islam. It's that the Qur'an eliminates the possibility of such a correspondence by denying that Jesus was God. (More on this in a later chapter.)

Yet the comparison between Ramadan and all three of the church seasons yields us Christians the great benefit of being able to see how all of them—Christmas, Lent, and Easter—fit together as one. They make a dynamic whole, with Easter as their culmination. Christmas is our cry of gladness at God's coming into our midst, in the wonderful vulnerability of a baby's flesh. Lent is the heightened recognition of the vulnerability of our own sinful flesh. Finally, Easter is where we rejoice at God's transformation of that vulnerability in the body of his resurrection.

Yet maybe the greatest benefit of the comparison follows from our immersion in Ramadan itself: from just breaking bread with our Muslim friends. For Muslims and Christians alike, the common meal is the most powerful sign of the hoped-for blessing of God on all God's friends. For many Christians a taste of that blessing is already given in the Eucharistic meal. For Muslims the taste is given after sundown during Ramadan, where we feast together in anticipation of the heavenly banquet to come.

SEVEN *Hajj* and *Easter*

◆ Celebrating the Hajj in Rochester, New York ◆

Our car creeps along icy February roads. . . . At last, the bright lights of the party house. My wife, Peggy, bundled, gets out of the car gingerly, testing the footing. I come around to take her arm. Together, we totter through the falling snow.

Inside, the sudden warmth and the hubbub of children running, voices calling out welcome, embraces, jokes, smiles.

The *eid al adha*, the feast of the sacrifice, commemorating the end of the Hajj.

But in Rochester? New York?

The difference in climate is stark enough. No hot, blinding desert sun to be found in Rochester, last I looked. But there's a lot more than mere weather that separates Rochester from Mecca. Mecca, where no non-Muslims are permitted to set foot . . . Mecca of the giant stone structure known as the Ka'bah, the very center of Muslim worship and the navel of the world . . . Mecca, the destination of the yearly Hajj, the pilgrimage incumbent upon every Muslim to make at least once in his or her lifetime, and one of the Five Pillars of Islam.

What do we have here in Rochester instead? A "party house," of all places. Not exactly a substitute for the Ka'bah. No holy ground of any kind to be seen, outside or in. Men for the most part in business suits—none of them wearing the traditional Hajj garment for males, two pieces of unhemmed, white cloth wrapped around the body, symbolizing *ihram* or a state of purity and single-minded dedication to God. The Muslim women at the party house are wearing colorful national styles, not the sober garments required for Hajj. Some are in Western dress. A few aren't wearing a hijab or veil. Of course, there are the several non-Muslims now present, including my wife and me along with members of other inter-faith committees, and our local congressperson too, all of us "foreigners," not only warmly greeted at the door, not only treated to a sumptuous buffet meal (featuring goat meat), not only given a table of honor, but also encouraged to speak at the after-dinner ceremonies.

Yet as I look around the large dining area, I see one very Hajj-like feature. I see that representatives of all Rochester's Muslim communities are here tonight. African-American and Turkish Muslims, who normally worship in their own *masajid* or mosques, along with Muslims from the Middle East, from Pakistan and the Indian sub-continent, the groups associated with the Islamic Center—all of them are equally busy trying to corral their children, who are running every which way and mix with each other in glad abandon. The Hajj should have such a result, of bringing all Muslims together into one ummah.

Doggedly, I feel compelled to keep before me the question: What does this particular eid-al-adha dinner have to do with the Hajj at that moment concluding half-way around the world in Mecca? Doesn't the incongruity of celebrating eid-al-adha in Rochester defeat any effort, however sincere, to produce a unity that can take form only in one place, thousands of miles away?

The question perplexes me, but not so much that I forget how good a time I and apparently everyone else is having. The first group to come back from filling up their plates at the buffet tables attacks the meal with gusto. Conversations all around me are lively. While seated waiting my table's turn, I find myself talking to a man who emigrated from Iran twenty years ago. We deplore together the totalitarianism of the ayatollahs. Then I mention the bad news from Mecca I heard earlier that week: Nearly 250 Muslim worshipers were trampled in a stampede during one of the Hajj rites, the annual stoning of Satan. Hundreds more were badly injured. And this wasn't the first such stampede. Nor is it likely to be the last, I add, given the resigned way I'd heard the Hajj minister in Mecca speak about the incident on the news. The minister stated that he'd taken all the precautions he could. He'd installed crowd control procedures. He'd even instituted a quota system drastically limiting the numbers of pilgrims from each country. Yet human contrivance had manifestly failed. "And so," sighed the minister, "caution wasn't stronger than fate." In my mind's eye I could see the Hajj minister throwing up his hands, helplessly.

Feeling uneasy that I had seemingly put the Hajj or at least the authorities in charge of it in a bad light in my new friend's eyes, I hasten to add, "Well, actually, I'm critical because I'm jealous. I'd really love to go on Hajj myself and know I can't." Which is true. I conceived this romantic desire after reading Malcolm X's glowing account of his own pilgrimage to Mecca in *The Autobiography of Malcolm X.*

My new friend smiles at the idea, then addresses the crux of the problem. "It's the crowds, two million people or so. And the emotionalism. One reason is the danger of it—the expense is another, and of course the waiting, sometimes for years, because of the quotas—those are the reasons that I'm not in any hurry to go there myself."

I don't know what to make of my new friend's attitude. On the one hand, it seems perfectly reasonable. Who wants to be caught up in a mob scene like the one at the stoning of Satan, especially one that year after year takes its grim toll of pilgrims? 244 trampled this year; 14 in 2003; 35 in a 2001 stampede; in 1998, 180? On top of that to pay thousands of dollars in travel and other expenses for the privilege!

But isn't Hajj one of the Five Pillars of Islam? How can my friend claim title to his faith if he avoids one of its main commandments? If I'd known him better, I would have asked him right then and there.

By now it's our turn at the buffet. I take my place in the line, dishing out a generous helping of goat, the first time I've had such fare. I'm not usually so adventurous with food, especially meat. But I have a special motive. Here, at last, is a clear symbol of connection between the Hajj and tonight's festivities at the Rochester party house. In Mecca, earlier in the day, goat or sheep (sometimes a camel or cow or steer) would have been sacrificed by each family after the culminating gathering known as the Standing Ceremony. At the banquets following, the Hajj would be concluded.

I return to the table feeling a little less distanced from the great Hajj events, thanks to that one helping of goat.

A fragile connection indeed, but no more fragile than it is for any Muslim present tonight. Muslims would be much more conscious than I of how far this eid al adha celebration differs from the ones now in progress in Mecca. Especially conscious would be those few in the group tonight who are *Hajjis*—the name given in honor to those who manage to complete the Hajj. But no one, Hajji or not, seems disappointed by tonight's event or gloomily wishing he or she were elsewhere, even in Mecca. My friend, the Iranian, certainly isn't wishing such a thing.

Besides, there's a practical reason for extending the spirit of the Hajj beyond the physical bounds of Mecca, and beyond rites like the circling of the Ka'bah that are only valid there. Some Muslims are prohibited from going on Hajj, and were always prohibited, for reasons of expense or the difficulty of the journey or bad health. The Qur'an, not wishing to put insuperable burdens on people, prescribes alternative ways of fulfilling the Hajj obligation. Today, as recent events have tragically demonstrated, there is the added difficulty caused by sheer numbers. The quota system, limiting the number of pilgrims from each country to a percentage of the total Muslim population of that country, is the imperfect answer. The Hajj ministers of the future will have to defy fate and take even more drastic measures. Meanwhile, the worldwide population of Muslims, now at some one billion, three hundred million, is growing. As it does, the proportion of those who can actually fulfill the Hajj requirement will continue to shrink.

What will take its place? The better question is: What is already taking its place? Religious practices aren't the product of committees, not even of Hajj committees. They grow up from people's ways of building fruitful relationships with each other through God. So, back at the table, sampling goat (verdict: like lamb but more bones), I wonder whether I should look at tonight's festivities positively: not as a diluted version of the eid al adha, not as a poor second or third cousin, but as a vibrant expression of the Hajj spirit, a spirit sending up healthy shoots right in the midst of Rochester's snows.

I am about halfway through my dinner when a Muslim woman from Pakistan, the wife of a friend, also from Pakistan, brings her teenaged daughter over to talk to me. I was chatting with the girl's mother earlier, mentioning to her that I hadn't seen her daughter since she was a little child until this evening, and that I was amazed at how she'd grown. I said something about hoping I could talk to the daughter before the evening was out. Well, now I have my opportunity.

I'm struck at the start to find that the daughter, though clothed in a colorful *qameez* or outer garment, isn't wearing the hijab or veil. When I start talking with her, I realize I'm speaking with a young woman who belongs solidly to United States middle class culture. It's not just the command with which she speaks English, but the ease with which she handles my teasing and the subtle inflections of voice that indicate possession of common cultural reference points. Her mother is obviously very proud of her. I can see why. As a former high school teacher, I can judge a winner when I see one. I see a successful future written all over her daughter's uncovered face. But what form will that future take? How will it be shaped by the course of events in which, for many influential Americans, Islam represents a civilization in inevitable clash and conflict with the West?

The daughter, having done her filial duty, excuses herself in order to gab with a girlfriend, who in contrast is wearing the hijab. Very likely we have here another symbol, like the Hajj itself, in the process of being adapted and transformed by the new conditions in which Islam finds itself in North America.

I finish my meal as the speeches begin. The congressperson gives the keynote, not seeming at all fazed by children running at top speed in every direction. The congressperson goes straight to the theme uppermost on the minds of Muslims in the United States that winter, the U.S. government's attack on civil liberties, not only through the Patriot Act, but through other policies as well: the establishing of "free-speech zones" to keep protesters from spoiling presidential appearances, for example. "I was under the impression," says the congressperson, "that the Constitution intends the whole country to be a 'free-speech zone.'" The audience applauds vigorously. Representatives of other groups come up afterwards to greet the assembly. These include the groups to which I belong, the Muslim-Catholic Alliance and the Commission on Muslim-Christian Relations. Leaders of each of Rochester's masajid or mosques come forward, as do representatives of specific immigrant groups. But it's the last speaker who captures my attention, because he expresses a Muslim initiative that is the direct fruit of the events of September 11 and that I have been hearing about consistently since then from Muslim leadership both local and national.

This initiative involves a redirection of the ummah's vision of itself, to include an ummah made up of United States citizens. "The time has come," the spokesperson says,

> to think of ourselves less as immigrants who just happen to be in the United States and whose real homes are elsewhere. We don't want to lose our immigrant roots. But clinging to them as we have been doing means we are at the mercy of other people's decisions. Now we need to put our energies into becoming what we are already are and what we have chosen to be, citizens of the United States. Doing so means that we have to act like citizens, taking responsibility for ourselves and for our children. We have

to dedicate ourselves to working within this political system—flawed as it is—to make it better. Let us begin by educating ourselves about our candidates, making sure we all make an informed vote this November. And let us not make the same mistake we made in 2000.

The word "mistake" in this context is, as I've learned, a coded reference to the fact that in 2000 Muslims voted as a bloc for George W. Bush, on the strength of candidate Bush's religiosity and his apparently greater support for the peace process in Palestine. Afterward, most Muslims regretted their failure to have immersed themselves sufficiently in American history and politics to understand what each candidate actually stood for.

This speech ended, voter registration forms are handed out. My wife and I marveled afterward at how easily a religious celebration turned into an exercise in political consciousness-raising and direct action. Would that have happened in any but the most militant Christian church? Yet there was nothing remotely militant about this eid-al-adha gathering. The emphasis was on inclusion, rather than on the opposite. If this was militancy, then it was militancy directed not towards the promotion of one group over another, but towards the solidarity of all those embracing values indistinguishable from the values advocated by our own Constitution: rights to free speech, to privacy, to a fair trial—values very much in harmony with the Islam practiced by the Muslims gathered at the party house that night, an Islam based on salaam, an overarching peace based on each person's claim to be equal in God's eyes.

Generalizations are dangerous. I can't claim that all eid-al-adha dinners held outside Mecca this evening—even the dinners in progress right now in other U.S. Muslim communities—have the same joyful, inclusive tone as this one held in Rochester. But at least here, in one tiny, snowy spot on the globe, the spirit of Muslim unity—the spirit evoked and embodied by Hajj but given a special shape by a political climate in the U.S. currently suspicious of, if not hostile, in many places to Muslims—here, at least, the spirit of Muslim unity is alive and flourishing.

◆ Origin, Practice, and Importance of the Hajj ◆

Muhammad didn't invent the Hajj. Pilgrimage to Mecca was a longstanding custom of the region, held at the end of each lunar year during a period of truce. Bedouin tribes, normally at war with each other, would break off hostilities long enough to come to Mecca to worship their own deity among the 360 tribal deities enshrined within the Ka'bah.

The merchants of Mecca counted on the pilgrimage as a major source of income. Quite naturally they opposed the message delivered through Muhammad that God was not many but one and that the tribal deities were naught. The merchants along with the Bedouins also opposed the moral restrictions this one God sought to impose upon them. Opposition led to persecution and eventually to Muhammad's hijrah or emigration to Yathrib (later named Medina) in 622 CE. When Muhammad returned in triumph to Mecca in 630 CE, he cleansed the Ka'bah of its idols.

But "cleansing" didn't mean eradicating the Ka'bah or squelching pilgrimage. Muhammad restored both to what he considered to be their proper and prior function, to their service as prime symbols of unity for the ummah of humankind. The worship of idols was a corruption of practices that it had been given to Muhammad to restore.

The 360 idols having been swept away, what was revealed? What had they and their worship been concealing?

To the eyes of faith a series of powerful overlayings of worship of the one God emerged.

According to Muslim tradition, creation began where Mecca now lies. Subsequently the first Muslim and the father of all subsequent Muslims, Adam himself, built there an altar of worship of the one God, laying the foundation of the cube-like structure known now as the Ka'bah (which means "cube").

Later on, Hagar, Sarah's slave (the woman by whom Abraham had had his first-born son, Ishmael), having been expelled from Abraham's tribe by Sarah, wandered with babe in arms to this site. She ran frantically between two hills near Mecca looking for water for Ishmael. She found it at last bubbling up miraculously from a well underneath the place where she had laid the baby.

A few years later, Abraham came to Mecca in obedience to God's command that he sacrifice his first-born son. He and this son, whom Muslims identify as Ishmael, jointly agreed to this sacrifice. Abraham was about to kill his son when God intervened, and a goat or sheep was sacrificed in Ishmael's place. Abraham and Ishmael rebuilt Adam's house of God in commemoration of God's gracious mercy.

Muhammad purified this House, now renamed the *baitullah* or House of Allah (or more familiarly the Ka'bah), and towards the end of the Hajj in 632 delivered his farewell speech to the assembled Muslims in the plain of nearby Arafat.

These are the major events in the story of faith as Muslims remember it. These are the events they reenact, each Muslim once in his or her lifetime, during the same final days of the lunar year. Muslims circle the Ka'bah seven times. They run between the two hills, just as Hagar did, and they drink, just as she and Ishmael did, from the miraculous well. They sacrifice a goat or sheep in remembrance of God's mercy to Abraham and Ishmael, and on the plain of Arafat they listen to a speech from a senior Muslim figure who, standing in the place where Muhammad delivered his farewell speech, urges the pilgrims and all Muslims to be true to the new resolves and illuminations granted them by God during the Hajj.

These outward practices carry great symbolic weight. Not only do they connect the Hajji to the defining moments in the story of faith. They connect the Hajji also to the defining moment of his own existence: not what occurs in this life, but what will occur in the life to come.

Entering Mecca during Hajj is a foretaste of passing through death into judgment. The unsewn garment of two pieces of white cloth that men put on at a certain point at the beginning of Hajj is their burial shroud. (Women wear sober clothing including the Hijab or head scarf.) If they have not made their will, they make it now. Ritually deceased, all Muslims together forswear a range of activities symbolic of life: using perfume, harming animals (even insects), carrying weapons, cutting their hair or fingernails, and many more. Those on Hajj are in effect corpses, alive only now to God, crying *labbaika* or Here I am! throughout the week, just as they will do on the Day of Judgment. The Five Pillars are pressed into one. Witness, daily prayer, fasting, and almsgiving become the total expression of the person each moment of the day, rather than separate activities to be carried out in the course of a day or a season. Hajj is the epitome of *ibada* or service to God, and the Hajji is purely 'Abd or servant. Nothing of him or her is "left over." There is only Islam, self-surrender.

One has sympathy for the Hajj minister! There is nothing "violent" about the Hajj ceremony as such. Yet symbols are dangerous. Faith gives symbols a power over us that we cannot always see or control,

But faith also provides correctives.

One of them is the way the Ka'bah is indirectly reduced in importance by the Qur'an itself. The Qur'an doesn't tell this story explicitly. What the Qur'an does instead is hint at Muhammad's *mi'raj* or ascent through the seven heavens to the real Ka'bah, the real baitullah or House of Allah—the one that makes the Ka'bah in Mecca seem a pale copy. Combined with several other powerful but enigmatic Qur'anic verses pointing to Muhammad's visionary experiences—anomalous, because the verses of the Qur'an came down to Muhammad almost always as "auditions" or numinous voicings—this one hint became the starting point for later, more detailed accounts based on what Muhammad told his companions privately. The accounts differ in details, but in most of them Muhammad rides on the back of the heavenly steed *Buraq*, and with the angel Gabriel as his guide, advances all the way to the Heavenly House of Life in the seventh heaven, against which he finds the prophet Abraham resting. From there he is conducted "to within two bow-shots" (*sura al-najm* 53:8) of God's presence. There, following the example of his ancestor in faith, Abraham, Muhammad begins to bargain—not over the righteous of Sodom, this time, but over the number of times Muslims should be expected to gather each day for prayer. Muhammad mercifully whittles the number down from fifty to five.

The accounts of Muhammad's mi'raj form a key part of popular religiosity as well as of Sufi spirituality. The stories incite the imaginations of Muslims of all social classes to locate the ultimate center of their worship beyond what can be seen, even beyond the most holy objects and places. That ultimate center is God himself, in whose house and before whose throne each human being must eventually stand. We have here the Wali's way of adjusting what otherwise might be the excessive reliance on the 'Abd's physical compliance with the Hajj obligation.

As a foretaste of what it might mean to stand in that true Ka'bah, no story is better than one told about the great Sufi female saint, Rabi'a of Basra.

> It is related that Rabi'a was going to Mecca another time. In the middle of the desert, she saw that the Ka'bah had come out to welcome her. Rabi'a said, "I need the lord of the house. What am I to do with the house? Its power means nothing to me. What delight is there in the Ka'bah's beauty? What I need to welcome me is the one who said: 'Whoever approaches me by a hand's span, I will approach by an arm's span.' Why should I look at the Ka'bah?"[vii]

Islam's passionate resistance to idolatry means that not even the Ka'bah or pilgrimage to it can substitute for the purity of an islam like that shown by Rabi'a. From her perspective, the Hajj pilgrimage is not made to Mecca, nor to the Ka'bah, but to God. Mecca and the Ka'bah are means towards ends. To make them the principal or only focus of Hajj is to commit *shirk*. That is, it is to make God into a partner at best, and a rival at worst. In any case, it is to return to the worship of the idols Muhammad had cast out long ago.

Without the real Ka'bah sitting solidly in place in Mecca and without the commitment and personal sacrifice of the millions of Muslims concretely and fervently living out the call to solidarity with God and each other and making the actual pilgrimage, there could be no extension of the Hajj spirit beyond Mecca's geographic bounds. And there could be no way to imagine, with Rabi'a, a Hajj more perfect, more God-centered still. Like politics, all worship is local. If worship is spiritually detached from place and physical presence it quickly becomes mere mental exercise. Mecca, the Mecca of the Arabian desert, remains the hub of the universe, the navel of the world.

◆ Returning to Easter ◆

¡Jesús resuscitó! ¡Jesús resuscitó! ("Christ is risen! Christ is risen!")

I looked behind me to find who the shouter was, what it was all about.

I couldn't mistake him. It was Father Tim at last, late, bustling into the church from the back, his alb flung over one arm, and waving to us with his free hand. His mop of white hair stood up like a halo around his head and framed the broad, pink, grinning face beneath.

¡Jesús resuscitó!

Father Tim began to make his way down the side aisle toward the sacristy, shaking hands, slapping people on the back, patting the children, and gabbing, gabbing.

Father Tim's facial features and coloring contrasted dramatically with those of the Mexican *trabajadores migrantes* (migrant workers), some with families of small children, who'd been sitting patiently in the pews for a long time now, not knowing whether they'd have a priest and a Mass on this Easter day or not. Not even the migrants' chief pastoral caregiver, a nun from Mexico, knew the answer to that question. She'd come over to me some minutes before Father Tim's sudden arrival to ask if I had any information on his whereabouts. Had I seen him outside the church? Had I spoken with him during the week? Had he mentioned that for some reason he couldn't come today?

¡Jesús resuscitó!

Father Tim yelled it one last time before he disappeared into the sanctuary to vest. I admired and, yes, envied his easy command of colloquial Spanish, the result of years of missionary work in South America. But what most impressed me was the way Father Tim's proclamation of the Christian faith—because that's what *¡Jesús resuscitó!* is, the very heart and soul of the Gospel—had transformed the congregation. The migrants' previously impassive, stoical expressions had eased into smiles under the irresistible pressure of Father Tim's exuberance. The *Buena Nueva* (Good News) had penetrated their defenses and opened them to the central truth of our Christian experience: the truth that unites us with Christ in the joy of the Resurrection.

I've since thought about Father Tim's shouting out *¡Jesús resuscitó!* that Easter morning at the Mass for migrants. (The area to the west and east of Rochester is a major apple-growing district and is therefore a magnet for migrant labor.) Whenever I find myself in a muddle about what it means to be a Christian, I come back to the incident I've just described. It always steadies me. It always helps me cut through my frustration not only with the current divisiveness within the Catholic Church to which I belong, but also with the divisiveness among Christians generally over various "hot-button" issues: homosexuality, abortion, women's rights, the death penalty, the just war theory, and on and on. The statement made about the first Christian community in Jerusalem—"the whole group of those who believed were of one heart and soul" (Acts 4:32)—mocks our present condition. So does the claim we make in the Nicene creed (which not all Christians honor!) that the Church is "one."

Whatever the density of the gloom-cloud that might be following me around from day to day as I ponder the state of the Church (like the inky black cloud that used to hover over the head of cartoonist Al Capp's character Joe BFSTTLK in the 'Lil Abner comics), Father Tim's glad shout, *¡Jesús resuscitó!*, always penetrates it, clearing the air and letting in light.

The shout comes to my ear as I mentally return from the Hajj to the Christian celebration of Easter. And a welcome noise it is! For sure enough: A gloom-cloud begins to form over me as I compare the concrete ways Muslims express their unity in the Hajj with the apparent lack of such expression in Christianity.

Take pilgrimage, for example. I grudgingly admit that the custom hasn't quite died out in the Christian world. Christians in Latin America still make pilgrimages to holy sites, especially as a Lenten penance. In Europe and elsewhere, Christians make pilgrimages to the sites of Marian appearances. But I somberly note that such pilgrimages, valuable for the individual pilgrim as they might be, don't have the power and meaning of the Hajj. They are not physical expressions of the universality of faith and of the unity of humankind under God. I pretty much convince myself that the closest we Christians come to the Hajj is the unity that might be felt by pilgrims to St. Peter's in Rome. But the unity, I reflect grimly, is fractured from the start by Christian sectarianism. For all Pope John Paul's and others' efforts to foster ecumenism, pilgrimage to Rome tends to be the property of Roman Catholics.

After all, the effort itself to foster ecumenism is a sign that the opposite of ecumenism is the case, and has been the case for a long time: namely, the Church's brokenness. Two great splits have caused this brokenness: first, the schism between the Eastern and the Western churches culminating in 1054 CE when the papal legate laid a bull of excommunication against Patriarch Cerularius on the altar of the Hagia Sophia in Constantinople; and second, and farther reaching in its effects, the split between Rome and the Protestant reformers symbolized by the delivery of another papal bull of excommunication, this time against Martin Luther in 1521. It's true that since the Second Vatican Council important steps towards reestablishing unity among the divided churches have been made, but not even the most optimistic observer could say more than that there's a long road ahead of us still.

And yet . . . *¡Jesús resuscitó!*

It's Easter morning anywhere in the world. Or better: Easter mornings, since one consequence of the East-West schism is that the Eastern and Western churches reckon Easter by a different calendar.

Let not the gloom-cloud form! Joe BFSTTLK, begone! It's Easter morning, whenever we decide that Easter morning is to be.

What's important about Easter morning for all Christians everywhere is not the date itself or the precise way in which it is celebrated in a particular church. What's important about Easter morning and what makes it central for every Christian, the focus of Christian life of whatever stripe, is that . . . *¡Jesús resuscitó!*

We can say that phrase in any language we want, memorialize it within whatever rite our tradition has provided for us. As long as we acknowledge that Jesus died and rose again from the dead and that by so doing he opened up that unimaginably joyful possibility for all who believe in him, then, whether we are of the East or the West, whether Reformed or Roman Catholic, we are one. We're one not by any power of charity that we can generate, but by the power of the Resurrection itself. Our perpetual divisiveness cannot overcome what God has done for us in Jesus Christ (though sometimes we act as if we wished it could).

The oneness God in Jesus Christ has gained for us isn't uniformity, however. Christians were never meant to be carbon copies of each other. God has never wanted that for us any more than he has ever wanted it for Muslims.

The point of experiencing the Hajj and bringing this experience back to Easter is likewise not to force a comparison or project a uniformity with Islam that does not and probably should not exist. The point is to enable us Christians to look at our own symbols of unity with fresh eyes—in this case with the eyes of our Muslim brothers and sisters.

One thing we see through those eyes is the opportunity both religions afford us of celebrating the unity of our respective faiths under a sign I'd at first rejected, the sign of universal pilgrimage. I'd thought such a sign applied to Christians in a fractured way only. But not so! Geographically focused on Mecca, for Muslims; geographically focused on the local church, for Christians, the sign of pilgrimage identifies both. For both Muslims and Christians what is celebrated under this sign, whether at Hajj or at Easter, is the promise and foretaste of new life after death. For both religions the celebration is shot through with joy. For this reason Easter Sunday gives the true note of Christian Hajj, with its Easter outfits, its special songs, its churches crowded with Christians who might keep their distance at other times of the year but for whom Easter sounds a call too sweet to be resisted. Everyone together, the piously practicing Christians and the nominal ones, the veterans and the newly baptized, the old and the young, *trabajadores migrantes* and their tardy Anglo priest, find once again their true home, their place of fundamental orientation in their life pilgrimage.

The fullness of unity hasn't happened yet, of course: not for us and not for Muslims. It may not happen until God gathers both of us in for the last time. As I call to mind the migrant workers and their families sitting in their pews awaiting a priest who, for all they knew, might never arrive at all, I get an image of a profound patience that could teach all of us, Muslims and Christians alike, how to behave in the meantime. Neither forcing a unity nor despairing of it, but instead accepting the apparent delay as an occasion for hope, knowing in our bones that the Word is on its way:

¡Jesús resuscitó!

EIGHT *Jihad* and *Fighting the Good Fight*

◆ A Courageous Muslim ◆

I found out the real meaning of Jihad not long ago at a large evening gathering of the progressive community of Rochester. The purpose of the meeting was to focus opposition to the Patriot Act of the George W. Bush administration. A number of speakers were to address the topic once we'd finished the delicious potluck supper.

Among those speaking out against the Patriot Act was Yasmin, a Muslim friend from Bangladesh and now a U.S. citizen.

As soon as she got behind the podium, Yasmin explained that, unlike the previous speakers, who had talked from the steps below, she had deliberately sought the podium's protection. "I need all the help I can get," is the way she put it.

Yet her voice was strong and did not betray her. She made a riveting figure, with her Hijab or veil and qameez and *shalwar* or flowing outer garments contrasting with the casual Western clothes worn by the men and women who had spoken before her.

Yasmin's message was riveting as well. She explained how the Patriot Act posed a special threat to her family, to her Muslim sisters and brothers, and to the health of the country of which she was now a citizen. In her view, the Patriot Act was a direct assault on the Bill of Rights as well as on the UN Charter of Human Rights.

Yasmin wasn't speaking just for herself. She wanted to bring home to us the way that the Act had affected the Muslim community of Rochester: and specifically the fear in which the 17,000 Muslims in the Rochester area were living as a result of interviews of local Muslims already conducted by the FBI and the INS. Recently there had been raids on Muslim-owned businesses by the FBI. Yasmin attributed the fact that so few Muslims (only one other, besides herself and her husband) were present that evening to this fear. She wasn't blaming her absent sisters and brothers. She was using their absence to make her point: The Patriotic Act has had a chilling effect on Muslims' confidence in their own adopted country's welcome of them. Moreover, she said, the Patriot Act represented a betrayal of the value of human dignity that Yasmin and other Muslims had come to the United States to share, support, and help nurture. That value, she explained, was an integral part of Islam itself.

Paradoxically, the Patriot Act had brought her into company with people with whom previously she would have had little to do. She and I and others have often talked about the reverse effect of government initiatives whose main if not stated intent is to freeze debate and even to aggravate cultural and religious differences. The initiatives exert this reverse effect by galvanizing people's deepest convictions in acts of conscious opposition. Yasmin's own act of conscious opposition touched and inspired all of us. Her act also prompted a question in our hearts—or at least it did so in mine: Will I be able to stand at that or a similar podium if or when the Patriot Act begins to affect directly the lives of people in my own social group? in my own church? in my own family?

Yasmin's gesture of conscious opposition inspired another question in me as well, not about myself but about her. What was the basis of her decision to expose herself in this way, as a woman and as a Muslim, in a friendly setting to be sure, but one in which she and her husband and one other person were the only Muslims present—perhaps the only ones who dared to be present? Her decision didn't come out of nowhere, didn't suddenly materialize on that very evening. Her decision had a history and a source.

A source in Jihad.

The fact that it took me a while to trace this source shows how strong a hold the news media's definition of Jihad as Holy War had on me. Yasmin's behavior that evening had been courageous, yes. But in no way could it be seen as violent. So how could Jihad have been at the base of it?

I gradually fought clear of the Jihad-violence equation by talking with my Muslim friends about their own understanding of Jihad and by studying the way the word is used in the Qur'an and in Muslim tradition. Only then could I see Yasmin's behavior in its proper perspective.

Jihad is one of the key words in Islam's powerful ethical lexicon. Its basic definition is no more and no less than to strive towards a righteous aim, and to put all one's energies and talents into the achievement of that end. The ethical imperative contained in Jihad is directed to the believer's heart, but the test of the Jihad's genuineness is the effect of the believer's subsequent behavior on the wellbeing of the ummah. Jihad has nothing to do with violence, with the deliberate and indiscriminate infliction of pain and suffering, with the victimizing and dehumanizing of others. Jihad has everything to do with courage and self-sacrifice. Yasmin to a T.

It wasn't that Yasmin called attention to herself or to Jihad that evening at the meeting of progressives. When I asked her some weeks afterwards if she felt that Jihad described her effort that evening, she admitted that it did, but with the characteristic disclaimer that she "hadn't done much, really." In part, this was Yasmin's modesty speaking. But not modesty alone. Speaking also was a deep understanding of human weakness, an understanding which is itself a key part of Jihad. To believe that we could judge for ourselves the quality of our own motive would be to commit *istikbarun*, arrogance, literally, "making oneself big, puffing oneself up." Jihad, rightly conceived, begins with an examination of conscience and a purging, or at least a candid acknowledging, of the self-interest that afflicts many if not most actions, even (or most especially) those carried out in the name of good causes.

No, Yasmin's act of Jihad did not presume on some supposed inherent virtue of her own. Nor did it presume on claims of religious pedigree: that because by tradition and ritual practice she belongs to the ummah of Muhammad she must necessarily be embodying Jihad whenever she speaks or acts on behalf of that community, regardless of the arguments or methods used or advocated. A good cure for this second presumption would be those many verses of the Qur'an that speak in harsh condemnation of *munafiqun* or hypocrites. Only God can judge the purity of our motives and the morality of our actions. Obviously, we have to make our own judgments about what we will do or not do in God's name. But our final decisions always cast us on God's mercy. A merciful God always favors merciful restraint in God's creatures.

Yet from my own perspective Yasmin's Jihad rang true. My proof would be her nonviolent witness to human dignity in the face of what she and many others believe to be an assault on it by the U.S. government, an assault directed, at the present moment, with greatest intensity upon those espousing Islam, but by no means limited to them. Her Jihad was in reaction to an attack on humanity itself. This follows from the fact that the Muslim hands him or herself over to God, not to the state (that is, to a certain "tribe" as opposed to other, competing ones). Only God can grant the Muslim the freedom to become what he or she is meant to be: God's servant and the servant of God's creation. To the extent that a government can enable this development, or at least not impede it, it deserves a Muslim's cooperation and support—and even the Muslim's Jihad in its favor. In this way, Yasmin's behavior that evening can be seen as Jihad in favor of the Bill of Rights and of an America that honors those rights. But when a government subjects even its citizens (to say nothing of those with visas or visa applications) to secret searches; when it imprisons them without due process; when it denies them an attorney, this is to attack those human rights. Such governmental behavior must be resisted in whatever country it appears, including countries governed by so-called "Muslim" regimes.

If this is Jihad, then may I myself be given the strength to embrace it!

◆ The True Meaning of Jihad ◆

Perhaps the most surprising thing to say about Jihad is that, until about a century ago, it did not have anything like the importance, either for Muslims or for Westerners, that it does now—and certainly very little of the scariness.

As mentioned earlier, the word in Arabic simply means to "struggle, to strive in a righteous cause." There is nothing mysterious or sinister about the word. It does not mean "fight"—there is another word for that, *qital*. So "Holy War" is a bad translation. Jihad really refers to Islam's asceticism, its emphasis on self-discipline. The point of such self-discipline is twofold: first, the cleansing of personal motive and, second, the dedication of oneself to active service for the betterment of the ummah. But ummah in this case is conceived very broadly. Its borders are political rather than religious. Jihad envisions a social order based on Qur'anic prescriptions of legal equality and of political salaam or permanent peace among tribes or groups that otherwise would be in perpetual conflict. Jihad does not envision the forced conversion of non-Muslim minorities. Jihad undertaken for selfish, destructive, or sectarian motives is strictly forbidden both in the Qur'an and in the subsequent legislation of the early Muslim centuries.

Jihad directed outwards, towards the defense or establishment of peaceful political order, has taken many forms, however. Ever since the hijrah or Emigration from Mecca in 622 CE, and continuing up to our day, these forms have answered to complex socio-political factors. Jihad as used in the Qur'an, for example, refers for the most part to the mobilization of believers to support and fight in the wars carried on by Muhammad to protect the new ummah from its enemies in Mecca and from certain Jewish and Bedouin tribes in and around Medina (the city where Muhammad found refuge after the hijrah). The issue for the new ummah wasn't only that these groups were hostile. Out-and-out opposition would have been bad enough. The main issue was that these groups were treacherous. If they were from distant tribes, they would make treaties of peace which they'd then break. If they were, or appeared to be, Muslims already, they would stab the new ummah in the back by slander, by failure to supply promised support, and by secret collusion with outsiders. Jihad is evoked with special vehemence against this latter group, called munafiqun or hypocrites.

In all such instances, Jihad is envisioned as defensive in nature. It is a method of last resort when efforts to secure peace treaties fail, either because the young ummah's enemies refuse to make treaties or because the enemies betray them once made. In the century after Muhammad's death, during Islam's rapid expansion east towards the Oxus River and west towards Spain, Jihad rallied Muslims in support of the caliphs' armies. This is the period in which the provisions for "just war" were worked out by Muslim legalists, basing their strictures on Qur'anic verses prohibiting the killing of non-combatants and allowing for the protection of non-Muslims, especially Jews and Christians, in Muslim-dominated countries.

But even as the rules for Jihad as warfare in service to the ummah were being worked out, notions of Jihad as the struggle of conscience were being elaborated as well. This is the period of the following famous hadith or story about Muhammad: On coming home from a raiding party, Muhammad is reported to have said, "We have now returned from the Lesser to the Greater Jihad." Asked to clarify the difference, Muhammad replied: "The Greater Jihad is the Jihad against oneself." Emphasis on the Greater Jihad reflects the parallel development of Muslim spirituality: the emergence of Esoteric (spiritual) Islam in union with Exoteric (political) Islam.

Yet as important as the concept of Jihad during the early Muslim centuries might be, the concept itself was ancillary to other practices and ideas in Islam. What brought about a change in Jihad's status was Western penetration into formerly Muslim-controlled lands through war and colonialism. By the end of the nineteenth century, the ummah was faced, for the first time in its history, by a culture that threatened to inundate it. Though the Muslim world had been invaded before, by the Mongols and the Turks, it had managed to absorb these invaders. The Mongols and Turks, while dominating their areas of conquest, became Muslims themselves. They added their talents to Muslim civilization and enriched it. But in the case of the West, it seemed more likely that Islam itself would be absorbed. In reaction to this ominous possibility, Jihad received new emphasis. In extremist thought, it became something like a sixth pillar of Islam: even a value transcending all others. In view of what extremists feared to be the imminent collapse of the ummah—the ummah whose preservation had been decreed and sanctioned by God—what else was called for but Holy War, apocalyptic struggle in the ummah's defense?

Extremist thought has been rejected by the vast majority of Muslims, however. Yasmin is typical of them. For her and many like her, Jihad refers to a struggle for peaceful co-existence and mutual understanding in a pluralistic world. There are many verses of the Qur'an that support this attitude. Like the extremists, though, Yasmin and all other Muslims today must wrestle with the term Jihad as they never did in the past. The questions now before Muslims are: Is Jihad to shrink to a principle of violent self-assertiveness, hardly distinguishable from self-destructiveness? Or is it to keep its original meaning— that of struggle to preserve and extend a just political order, an order seen now as pluralistic, not dominated by any one nation or religious group, not even by Muslims themselves?

The question concerns us in the West just as much. How Jihad will be defined in the decades to come, whether as the extremists define it or as Yasmin does, will depend greatly on Western sensitivity to the unfolding crisis within Islam. Will our actions exacerbate that crisis? Or will our actions allow understanding of our common responsibilties as *kalifa* or stewards ("caliphs") of God's creation?

The answer depends in great part on our own willingness to struggle—to perform Jihad—for a just society. Those gathered at the meeting of progressives where Yasmin spoke didn't use the word Jihad for their own commitment to that cause any more than Yasmin did, but they could have. Maybe they should have. Maybe doing so would have helped dispel the notion that Jihad is something belonging to Muslims exclusively and that its only significance is a destructive one.

◆ Christian Jihad ◆

If progressives have reason to embrace the concept of Jihad as their own, why not Christians too? Why can't we speak of a "Christian Jihad"?

The idea is by no means absurd. We Christians actually share with Muslims a concept very much like Jihad. It's not identical. It has a different focus, and a different development. But its similarity in other ways gives Christians solid ground for collaboration with Muslims, both in our spiritual practices and in the effort to build a just and therefore an inclusive society, one that gathers and nurtures all God's children, whatever their religion or non-religion.

Still, the notion of Christian Jihad takes getting used to. Christianity considers itself a religion of peace, after all,

Christ, unlike Muhammad, never led troops into battle. In the garden, Christ told Peter to put down his sword. The early church in Acts never took up arms against attacks by leaders of the synagogues and later by the Romans, but either endured, and celebrated, martyrdom, or else fled to areas like Antioch where they could worship in relative peace. What do such long-suffering attitudes have to do with a Qur'anic verse like the following?

> Not on the same level are those believers who sit at home (unless they're disabled) with those who struggle [*jahiduna*—the context indicates that "struggle" here means "fight"] in God's cause with their wealth and their lives. . . . (*sura al-nisa'* 4:95)

We could add too that when the New Testament does talk about warfare, it does so in a spiritualized, even cosmic sense:

> For our struggle is not against enemies of blood and flesh, but against the rulers, against the authorities, against the cosmic powers of this present darkness, against the spiritual forces of evil in the heavenly places. (Eph. 6:12)

Doesn't such a passage and the whole tenor of the New Testament turn a phrase like "Christian Jihad" into an oxymoron?

To answer this question, and setting aside for a moment the apparent contradiction between armed Jihad and Chistianity as a religion of peace, let's remember, first, that Jihad also includes the Greater Jihad, the purifying of motive, and the subsequent dedication of oneself to service for the well-being of the ummah, conceived of as the whole of humankind. This is Yasmin's understanding of the word. Then let's look at our own Scriptures to see if we can find a parallel emphasis on struggle in service to the building of God's kingdom of right relationships.

I start with a Gospel passage that sets up the motive for Christian Jihad: the need to overcome our fear of following Christ.

> They were on the road, going up to Jerusalem, and Jesus was walking ahead of them; they were amazed, and those who followed him were afraid. He took the twelve aside again and began to to tell them what was going to happen to him, saying,
>
> "See, we are going up to Jerusalem, and the Son of man will be handed over to the chief priests and the scribes; and they will condemn him to death; then they will hand him over to the Gentiles; they will mock him, and spit upon him, and flog him, and kill him; and after three days he will rise again." (Mk. 10:32–34)

The disciples' instinct, and our own too, is to grow weak in the knees and lag behind when we realize what discipleship costs: nothing less than the Cross.

It's precisely to counter this reaction that Christian Jihad is born.

But what exactly is Christian Jihad? One thing it's clearly not is proud toughness. It is not a muscular reliance on one's own determination to "take it," even if the "it" means bloody martyrdom. The lines that follow the lines just quoted from Mark's Gospel make that point clear. In these lines Jesus easily dismisses James' and John's bold claim to be able to muscle their way to heaven by drinking Jesus' cup. Jesus says to them (10:38): "You do not know what you are asking."

This same tough-talking pair, James and John (along with Peter) can not even keep awake with Jesus during his agonizing night in Gethsemane. Yet here in Gethsemane is where Christian Jihad first appears—not as an attribute of the disciples, however, but of Jesus himself!

The key passage is Luke 22:44. "In his anguish he prayed more earnestly, and his sweat became like great drops of blood falling down on the ground." The word "anguish" translates the Greek word *agonia* (hence the "agony in the Garden"). *Agonia*, referring to a struggle for victory, to a contest, as well as to fear of an impending event, is our key for understanding Christian Jihad: What our English versions of the New Testament translate as "in anguish" (or sometimes "in agony") the Arabic version in my possession[viii] translates as *jihadin*, a form of the noun jihad.

What this means is that for Arabic-speaking Christians, Jesus' inner battle not to waver in his faith in God's plan for him and for all humanity—despite the horror of the death he'll soon be subjected to—is truly a Jihad, indeed the model of Christian Jihad. Personal firmness, vigorous moral resolution of the highest order is obviously called for. But more necessary still is trustful openness to a divine love whose methods and ways utterly confound our expectations—and our fears.

Such trustful openness, such vigorous persistence—in a word, such Christian Jihad—is communicated to the disciples only after the Resurrection. For it's then that the community formed through the Holy Spirit is given the capacity to supply what was missing in James, John, and Peter at Gethsemane. We could even say that the capacity for Christian Jihad is the Spirit's special mark. Before the Spirit's coming, we and the disciples fall behind in fear, we fall asleep. Come the Spirit, we are fearlessly alive to the Spirit's call, even running in answer to it.

Christian Jihad is articulated in the preaching of the early church, and especially in the letters of Paul. We can hear it emerge, for example, in Paul's exhortation to the Romans that they "struggle" with him in prayer:

> I appeal to you, brothers and sisters, by our Lord Jesus Christ and by the love of the Spirit, to join [Greek *sunagonisasthai*, Arabic *tujihadu*] me in earnest prayer on my behalf, that I may be rescued from the unbelievers in Judea and that my ministry to Jerusalem may be acceptable to the saints. (Rom. 15:30-31)

The Arabic word for "joining in earnest prayer" in this passage—*tujihadu*—is simply a form of the verb that the noun Jihad is based on. What may be harder to see is how Christ's Jihad in Gethsemane has much at all to do with a prayer Paul requests from the Roman congregation. If we examine Paul's request more closely, however, we discover that the connecting link is the prayer's content. What Paul is asking from God, in his own prayers and in those he hopes the Roman congregation will say for him, is exactly what Jesus prayed for: trustful openness to God's care not only for the one praying, but for others. Paul sees himself facing persecution and even death when he returns to Jerusalem. He asks for an act of Jihad on the part of others that will strengthen him in the Jihad he himself must soon perform. By praying for him, the Roman congregation will participate in Paul's own strengthening of purpose. They will share in the Jihad.

Unlike Jesus in his appeal to James, John, and Peter in Gethsemane, though, Paul has reason to believe that the Roman congregation will honor his request that they "join in earnest prayer on my behalf." Jihad emerges here in its communal form. The Christian *agon* or Jihad has its private origin in each person's encounter with the risen Christ. But its ultimate purpose is for the building up of the community, a community potentially embracing the whole world.

This building up will be, in Paul's mind, the work of spiritual warriors. That's clear from a passage like the following:

> Fight the good fight [Greek *agonizou ton kalon agona;* Arabic *jahid jihada-l imayni-hsana*] of the faith; take hold of the eternal life, to which you were called and for which you made the good confession in the presence of the many witnesses. (1 Tim. 6:12)

Paul's imagery for Christian Jihad is usually athletic—running is his favorite metaphor. Imagery of physical competition, hinted at in the example above and explicit in Paul's references elsewhere to boxing and wrestling and even gladiatorial combat, is frequent also. But battle imagery attracts him too. The clearest example of this type is found in the passage from Ephesians cited earlier, where Paul exhorts his audience to "put on the whole armor of God . . . for our struggle is not against enemies of blood and flesh . . . but against the cosmic powers of this present darkness. . . . In 2 Tim. 4:7 Paul combines both athletic and battle imagery when he says of himself: "I have fought the good fight, I have finished the race, I have kept the faith." The difference between Paul's athletic and battle imagery reflects different perspectives on the same Jihad: athletic when Paul looks forward to the goal, militaristic when he considers the external opposition, whether from persecution by Roman authorities or from cosmic powers, that the young church is forced to confront.

The battle imagery for Christian Jihad stays safely that— imagery—in Paul's letters.

After October 28, 312 CE, however, the battle is no longer fought in figures of speech or in the cosmic spheres, but in flesh and blood—just where Paul, in Ephesians 6:12, said that it was *not* to be fought.

For on that day, at the Milvian Bridge, Constantine defeated Maxentius, his greatest rival for sole control of the Roman Empire, thereby turning Jihad into Holy War.

Constantine is supposed to have had a dream on the night before the battle. In his dream he saw in the sky the initial Greek letters of Christ's name. Then he heard a voice say, "By this sign you will conquer." Fatefully inspired, he had the letters painted on his own and his soldiers' helmets. Constantine attributed his subsequent victory to the Christian God. In 312 now-emperor Constantine issued the Edict of Milan, ending all persecution of Christians. Christianity didn't become the official religion of the empire until 395, after Constantine's death, but Christianity had won the emperor's favor, with consequences for the meaning of Christian Jihad—not to mention concepts and practices even more central to Christianity, like the definition of the Trinity and state support of the clergy—that we are still wrestling with today.

Because as we move from Muslim Jihad to its Christian cousin, we discover that the differences between the two notions are perhaps not as stark as we thought. Both of our religions understand very well and rightly value the importance of the Greater Jihad, of what St. Paul called "fighting the good fight" and what prophet Muhammad called "the Jihad against oneself." The Lesser Jihad, the Holy War in flesh and blood, has put its bloody stamp on both faiths, earlier in the development of Islam than in the development of Christianity, but with problematic results for both religions. We see nearly every day in the news evidence of the tragic distortion of Islam by suicidal Jihadi extremists. Harder for us to admit to is the tragic distortion of Christianity by our own Crusaders. Think of the way Holy War rhetoric dominated Pope Urban II's call for the First Crusade in 1095. The Pope urged the knights of Europe to exterminate the Turks ("an accursed race, a race utterly alienated from God") and to free the Holy City of Jerusalem from the hands of the infidels.[ix] While we haven't called for this sort of Jihad in centuries, we Christians still have to take the measure of the long history of our enlistment of God on the side of our armies. President George W. Bush's apparent slip of the tongue in pronouncing the "war against terror" a "crusade" evokes an attitude that both Constantine and Pope Urban II would have instantly understood—and endorsed.

There will be Muslims and Christians who will accept the unlimited embrace of the Lesser Jihad as God's will in the cosmic battle of good versus evil. Others will see it as a sign of our brokenness, of our recurring attraction to violent solutions to our difficulties and differences.

For me, the Greater Jihad is what I share gladly and gratefully with Yasmin, and with most (but not all) Muslims as well as with most (but not all) Christians—along with most (but not all) other children of God—with all those who fix before them the dignity of each human being as the object of their Jihad or striving.

NINE '*Isa* and *Jesus*

◆ Double Identity ◆

'Isa is the name used in the Qur'an to refer to Jesus.

But is it to the same Jesus—to "our" Jesus—that the Qur'an is referring?

The answer is: Yes—and no.

The two names, Jesus and 'Isa, refer to beings who are the same and yet utterly, profoundly, different. For Christians, Jesus is Son of God. For Muslims, 'Isa is simply a prophet (though a great one), and explicitly and emphatically *not* the Son of God. Yet the Qur'an insists it is talking about the same person as Christians are. It explains the conflict of identity by saying that we Christians don't truly know our man. And that we've even been unjust to him by treating him as if he were more than a man.

I was aware before I met 'Isa in the Qur'an that I would be heading into trouble over this point. Yet I was prepared to allow the Qur'an and my Muslim friends to see my Lord and Savior as a prophet only. I'd simply keep my own counsel. And stay away from discussion of our differences because obviously they could never be resolved. Jesus was Jesus and 'Isa was 'Isa and that was it.

What I didn't reckon on was the way the Qur'an would induce me to grow fond of 'Isa and to admire him, just as Muslims themselves do. And on the way this admiration would reveal to me a certain narrowness in my relationship with 'Isa's counterpart, Jesus. My understanding of Jesus—the "Christian" Jesus—while doctrinally impeccable, had begun to show musty signs of possessiveness. As if the Son of God were knowable only within the terms of the Christian cult dedicated to him. As if Jesus were a kind of mascot whom no one else except his Christian keepers should think of claiming as their own and of dressing up in different colors.

What opened me to 'Isa was my Muslim friends' genuine love of him. And this is the approach I suggest to other Christians as well. Through Muslims' love of the Qur'anic 'Isa, we can find ourselves challenged by what sharing in such love reveals to us about our own faith. And challenged to ask with fresh urgency what is meant by saying that we are Christians, followers of God's Son, the Risen One, in the light of the fact that our Muslim friends are equally firm in their conviction that this beloved Son is no more and no less than a prophet—yet no less beloved for that.

Suppose, for example, that our Muslim friends have sat down with us so that we can read with their help a section of the Qur'an's second chapter or sura, *sura al-baqarah* or The Heifer. And in the course of our conversation we come upon the verse where 'Isa is mentioned in the Qur'an for the very first time:

We gave Moses the Book [i.e., the timeless revelation containing God's essential teachings for humankind, the same teachings enjoining praise and service that God has issued to humankind through all messengers but with special clarity since Moses] and caused to follow after him a succession of messengers. For example, we gave 'Isa the son of Mary clear signs and strengthened him with the holy spirit. But isn't it the case that whenever a messenger comes from me with a message you don't like, that you puff yourselves up, calling some of those messengers imposters while killing others? (2:87)

No matter what the setting, we couldn't miss the assumption in this passage that Jesus is regarded by Muslims as one in a succession of "messengers": an honored one, clearly, and yet in a certain way inferior to Moses, who is cited here as the first to receive the "Book." We'd probably be tempted to conclude either that Muslims and Christians simply aren't talking about the same person when they refer to Jesus/'Isa or that there is some kind of obstinacy on Muslims' part that induces them to distort the identity of Jesus, reducing the Son of God to a member of the prophetic guild—a respectable group to be sure, but no more than a group of human beings.

Getting to the passage with the help of Muslim friends makes it hard to be so dismissive.

Getting to it with the help of Muslim friends means sharing the Muslim view of their treasured prophet. It means approaching 'Isa, not objectively (if indeed such a thing is possible), but subjectively, through friendships and perhaps, by means of those friendships, through a deepening attraction to this strange text.

Getting to know 'Isa in this way shouldn't lessen our aware-ness of 'Isa's immense differences from Jesus. Instead, it should persuade us to hold both persons in our hearts at the same time, as both equally "true."

The contradiction is obvious, and it would be unnatural not to feel discomfort trying to bridge it in this way. How can the contradiction be sustained, psychologically and intellectually— not to mention spiritually? How can we believe that Jesus both is and is not the Son of God?

I can't answer for others, obviously. But in my own case a funny thing happened as my tutor Omar and I were sitting cross-legged at the back of the Islamic Center's masjid or prayer area during one period of those Saturday afternoons. Omar was reciting the Qur'anic verses about 'Isa and I was trying to imitate him, in the time-honored way of both acquiring a skill and of imbibing the spirit in which to employ it. I was getting to know 'Isa as if I were a Muslim child sitting with my master in a *madrasah* or Qur'anic school, or even at home, at my mother or father's knee.

We had reached the later references to 'Isa in *sura al-baqarah*, and further on in *sura al-nisa'* or Women and then especially in *sura al-ma'idah* or The Table Spread (the one that contains perhaps the richest Qur'anic characterization of 'Isa). To my surprise, the psychological, intellectual, and spiritual crisis that I'd half-expected and half-feared never came to pass. Not even when we came to those passages of the Qur'an that are explicitly anti-Christian, the ones that deny, for example, that God could ever have had a Son, or that God could ever be Three.

I used to say to myself, while we were working through such passages, *Surely something in me will revolt at these statements, since I don't in fact believe them and since they directly contradict what I do believe.* Yet all I could find in my heart was peace. It was as if the heavy weight of doctrinal confrontation between Islam and Christianity had been transformed, made somehow light or had been shifted somewhere else, perhaps upon Someone else.

Sometimes, when Omar had interrupted the session so that he could join the other men when a prayer time coincided with our hour together, I would sit by myself musing and often talking with Jesus—and maybe a little bit also to 'Isa as well.

I would say things like this:

Well, I don't know what any of this means, that there is this 'Isa and that this 'Isa is both you and not-you. I don't know what it means that as I look around this masjid, I don't see a single sign or symbol of you: no cross, no painting, no stained glass window, no altar—and yet here I am talking with you, in some ways more comfortably than I'm able to do inside one of your own churches. I don't know what it means that it's because of you I'm here in the first place— that I wouldn't have come here if I hadn't been baptized, if I hadn't tagged along when my wife was having training in Christian nonviolence, if I hadn't watched the War in the Gulf and hadn't felt sure that this war, and all wars, contradict and abuse your will for us. I don't know what it means that you seem to want me to let go of—or at least suspend—my understanding of you as Son of God. I don't know what it means that you want me to know you in another way, as my friends here know you, as great prophet, as 'Isa.

Then I'd shake my head, smiling inwardly. *What do you have in mind by playing this game with me? What's your purpose in leading me, your sheep, outside the fold where you're worshiped and into the fold where you're merely one of the flock yourself, though a very distinguished one?— assuming one can speak of a "distinguished sheep!"*

It never seemed to me that Jesus was less present just because his usual symbols were absent or because he was referred to by another name. But this presence-in-absence also never seemed a subterfuge, something given to my eyes but invisible to everyone else. As if Jesus had entered the Islamic Center in disguise or as if he had turned Omar and every other Muslim present into "anonymous Christians," worshiping Jesus in 'Isa without their consciously knowing it.

Of course, I could say that Jesus was present there in me. But what did that mean?

The only answer to that last question, if there was an answer, was to press on with my questions.

Who is this 'Isa who both was and wasn't my Lord?

◆ Who is 'Isa? ◆

One of the most poignant moments during my many conversations at the Islamic Center occurred when a Muslim friend said to me, "But we *love* Jesus." His tone was hurt, aggrieved, as if he had been accused by one friend of disloyalty to another.

I believed I knew why my friend responded that way. The Qur'an speaks about Jesus—that is, 'Isa—in the warmest possible way. To no other prophet, not even to Muhammad himself, does God give the special qualities that he gives to 'Isa. Only 'Isa is born of a virgin through divine fiat and the holy spirit. Only 'Isa speaks in defense of his mother as an infant in the cradle. Only 'Isa breathes on clay birds, so that on living wings they fly away. Only 'Isa clairvoyantly predicts where certain items are stored in a home. Only 'Isa is able to raise the dead to life. Only 'Isa escapes death on the cross in order that he may appear, still alive, at the Last Judgment.

So, given the high respect, indeed, the honor 'Isa enjoys among Muslims, what are Muslims to make of the apparent lack of gratitude Christians show to such respect? And not only of our lack of gratitude, but also at times even of our outright hostility to any sort of Muslim claim to relationship with our Lord?

I didn't know how to comfort my friend. I'll admit that part of me—the part that always hopes there are easy solutions to complex problems—was tempted to say, "Well, that's all well and good, this love you Muslims say you have for Jesus, but you see, we Christians believe he's Son of God." As if the best I could have done was to pat my Muslim friend on the head, leaving him to his well-meaning but incurable benightedness. Fortunately a wiser part intervened and I kept my mouth shut!

But while I was of no use to my Muslim friend, my friend was useful to me. Thanks to his comment about 'Isa, and the passion with which he stated it, I began to wonder what 'Isa actually looked like through my friend's, through Muslim eyes. Why was it that what my friend saw there prevented him from seeing anything else in 'Isa than the prophet? More important and positive, what did he see in 'Isa himself—leaving aside, if I could, the inevitable doctrinal gulf between 'Isa and Jesus—that would make my Muslim friend love him?

An answer to the first question came much faster than an answer to the second.

What prevented my friend from seeing anything else in 'Isa but the prophet was the fact that "prophet" is what the Qur'anic 'Isa insistently claims himself to be. In one place the Qur'an presents 'Isa at the Last Judgment staunchly defending himself before God against the rumor that he ever claimed godhead in a trinity with God himself. 'Isa is in fact unusual among Qur'anic prophets in that he alone is seen constantly embroiled in controversy with a rival evaluation, in this case, with the Christian evaluation of himself as Son. Other prophets, including Muhammad himself, are seen by their detractors as less than what they claim to be—they are seen as charlatans, madmen, or mere "poets." Only 'Isa gets in trouble for being seen as more. Only 'Isa has to assert explicitly that it's quite enough to be a prophet in the Qur'anic mode, one who brings to his own people the same, simple, unchanging message of God's beneficence and mercy, just as Moses had brought it to his people in an earlier time, and Muhammad would bring it to his in the future.

The controversy challenging 'Isa's identity affects everything he says in the Qur'an. 'Isa is scarcely born before he's forced into controversy. Defense of his mother Mary's honor is the immediate motive. But the opportunity given him by this occasion to proclaim his own prophetic identity, as distinct from his alter-ego Jesus' claim, is the overriding one.

The controversy arises when Mary, having fled, all alone, to the desert to give birth to 'Isa, returns to town carrying the newborn child. The townspeople are scandalized. They remind Mary of her family's good repute. They point out, with malicious sarcasm, that her father never chased after prostitutes, nor was her mother a whore. Mary doesn't defend herself in words.

She pointed, instead, at her child. The townspeople said, "How are we supposed to talk with a child in a cradle?" But the child spoke up, "Hear this: I am a servant of God ['abdullah]. God has given me the message [literally, al-kitabah or "the book"] and has made me a prophet. He has made me blessed wherever I go, and he has commanded me to be faithful to prayer and almsgiving as long as I live. He has made me gentle and just with my mother, neither bossy nor irritable. So peace [salaam] is with me from the day of my birth to the day of my death till the day I shall be raised to life." Such a man was 'Isa, son of Mary. This is the truth, about which they [the various Christian sects] vainly dispute. (*sura Maryam* 19:29–33)

The Qur'an continues in this homiletic vein, warning listeners of the danger of paying attention to those disputes and of falling into the idolatrous belief in 'Isa's Sonship. As a result, we never find out how the townspeople received this extraordinary speech. But that's only to say that the Qur'an, here as elsewhere, treats narratives allusively. The story of Mary, the baby, and the townspeople has little value in itself except as it occasions urgently needed instruction about who this 'Isa is—and isn't.

If the Qur'an treats narratives allusively or even obliquely, it tends to do the same with theological language. At just those places where we Christians expect and demand theological clarity, the Qur'an tends to shy off, as if a proliferation of words at that point would merely add to what the Qur'an sees as a mare's nest. A case in point is 'Isa's final statement in the quotation above: "So peace (salaam) is with me from the day of my birth to the day of my death till the day I shall be raised to life." On the face of it, this statement seems in complete accord with the Nicene Creed: Jesus was born, died, and rose again to new life. But the accord is short-lived. What 'Isa doesn't assert with the expected clarity (his being at the time a new-born infant is no excuse!) is that this language fits a man, not God. Other verses in the Qur'an, themselves allusive and ambiguous, indicate that he did not die on the cross at all—rather it was someone else who ended up crucified. Just how or when 'Isa will die is another source of ambiguity. As for his rising to new life, that is no more nor less than what will happen to all the rest of us at the Last Judgment.

Yet for all its prickly sensitivity to Christian claims about Jesus, the Qur'an actually devotes only a relatively few verses to the subject. That fact alone can be disconcerting. *Why* isn't a question of primary importance to all Christians from the time of the Gospels till today—"who do you say that I am?" (Mt. 16:15)—why isn't this question treated with the thoroughness it deserves? Isn't there something unfair about the Qur'an's restriction of 'Isa's role to that of spokesperson against the Sonship of Jesus? The Qur'an refers to 'Isa's ministry of healing, for example, but only in passing. We never hear details. And as for the crucifixion, the most detailed account of Jesus' life as given in the Gospels, the Qur'an has frustratingly little to say. What, according to the Qur'an, happened to him on the cross, exactly? How did his replacement—if that is what the ambiguous words used in *sura al-nisa'* 4:157 refer to—get up there? What happened next? The Qur'an refuses to tell stories:

They did not kill him, nor did they crucify him. He [or "it"—the pronoun reference is unstated] only appeared to them. Those who disagree are full of doubt about the matter with no clear knowledge but swarm instead after vain conjecture. The only sure point is that they did not kill him.

And that's that!

But what's skimpy to me is more than enough to a Muslim.

How are we Christians to understand Muslim lack of interest in this essential point of our doctrine, in Jesus' death and resurrection? The usual explanation has to do, in part, with what the Qur'an actually says above: that Christians at this period had become wearisomely disputatious and hopelessly abstract in their accounts of who Jesus was, or at least that they could very plausibly have looked that way to Semitic people—like the Arabs—who were naturally drawn to concreteness. Besides, a strictly human Jesus uniquely gifted by God for prophethood answered the need expressed everywhere in the

Qur'an to oppose Bedouin polytheism. A "Son of God" seemed simply to muddy the waters, merely confirming the Bedouins in their stubborn belief in multiple deities.

So the speculation goes, and it's an interesting study. The real challenge, as suggested above, is to see this 'Isa who escapes death on the cross through Muslim eyes. Why do Muslims love this elusive figure?

I don't think the Qur'an alone can answer this question. Subsequent, post-Qur'anic legends about 'Isa fill out the Qur'anic picture. They speak of 'Isa as a great ascetic, wonder-worker, and Sufi saint. The legends clearly reflect fascination with 'Isa as well as a desire to weave bits of information about him both from the canonical Gospels and from apocryphal sources into a richly Muslim design. One could well feel love for this extra-Qur'anic 'Isa.

Even the Qur'anic passages already cited give hints of 'Isa's attractiveness. His charming filial loyalty as a newborn in speaking up for his mother and for prophethood—as Muslims understand it—is one such hint. His stout defense of his prophethood (and denial of his rivalrous Sonship) before God at the Final Judgment is another. Bracketing our Christian insistence on doctrinal correctness for a moment, we can see this 'Isa as admirably true to his setting within Islam. His unusual human status (son of Mary by the *ruhi-qudusi* or "holy spirit"—seen by Muslims not as a theological "person" but as mere expression of the power of God—) doesn't cause him to *istakbara* or "puff himself up" in arrogance. From the very cradle he knows exactly who he is, even then, wrapped in swaddling: a prophet—no less, but no more. He acknowledges his obligations to prayer and fasting—those obligations incumbent on any Muslim. He embraces the reward of his behavior: salaam, despite the opposition he, like any other prophet, will face. But in a touch that shows a becoming realism, he humbly accepts and pledges to honor the behavior proper to him even as a child: "He has made me gentle and just with my mother, neither bossy nor irritable."

That's 'Isa at the beginning of his career.

At the very end of it, standing before God at the Final Judgment, he is no less forthright, no less clear-eyed about himself, no less pliant to God's will. "You know what is in my heart," 'Isa says to God. "I do not know what is in yours. For indeed you know all hidden things." So speaks, with lifelong consistency, the human prophet of God.

Then this same human prophet adds: "I told humankind only what you bade me" (sura al-ma'idah 5:117). An echo from the Gospels challenges my complacency about who this 'Isa is—and isn't. For it's impossible for me to read that last ayah or verse without recalling what his counterpart Jesus says, in John 12:49-50:

> . . . for I have not spoken on my own,
> but the Father who sent me
> has himself given me a commandment about what to say
>   and what to speak.
> And I know that his commandment is eternal life.
> What I speak, therefore, I speak
> just as the Father has told me.

If I love the one for his fidelity to God and humankind in John 12, it's hard to refuse it to the other in sura ma'ida or The Table Spread, 5:117. To love Jesus and 'Isa is not—it goes without saying—to love the same person. So loving the one is very fundamentally different from loving the other. Yet in another sense loving is loving, in so far as admiration and gratitude are some of loving's essential ingredients. And since, as Paul says, "Love is patient; love is kind; love is not envious or boastful or arrogant or rude" (1 Cor. 13:4), how do I keep love in containers, doling it out in careful measure according to a prior decision about who deserves it and who doesn't?

My Muslim friend told me he loves Jesus—not 'Isa, but Jesus. Or did he mean 'Isa but said Jesus because he didn't think I'd recognize the name 'Isa? Or is it the will of God—of Jesus, and therefore of 'Isa, who always obeys God's will—that the two, Jesus and 'Isa, be loved in some profoundly complementary way? Only love itself could lead so persuasively to such an apparently contradictory conclusion!

◆ Returning to Jesus ◆

Getting to know and love 'Isa gives new meaning to the famous passage from Philippians 2:6-7, the one that describes Christ as one who "did not regard equality as something to be exploited," but instead "emptied himself, taking the form of a slave." I'd always been drawn to this passage as one of the profoundest formulations not only of who Jesus is, but also of what we can become by following him. Studying the Qur'an at the Islamic Center gave me a concrete opportunity to put the Philippians paradigm in practice by letting go or at least by relaxing my doctrinal grasp on Jesus as Son of God, so that I could know Jesus in another way, as Muslims know him, as great prophet.

Throughout the years that have followed my first lessons with Omar at the back of the masjid, I've never felt the least anxiety on Jesus' part—if I may put it that way—about Jesus' own particular emptying, the emptying of himself of divinity in the Muslim understanding of him as 'Isa. If God was ever worried or incensed or aggrieved about the doctrinal contradiction involved, God has never once manifested those reactions to me. If that sounds as if I'm suggesting a laissez-faire attitude towards religious difference on God's part, I also have to say that God seems equally on the side of restraint. Not once have I ever felt that as a result of my joyful discoveries about 'Isa or about any other aspect of Islam that God wanted me to do something drastic, like "change my religion" or "convert." God seems quite happy about my being and staying a Christian, with my continuing to see him in Jesus the Son.

But God also seems to want me to see in that Sonship more wonders than I'd been able to grasp before. Getting to know 'Isa has made me more sure than ever that being a Christian involves a kind of adventurousness, a certain kind of risk-taking. Loyalty to who we are: This is essential. So is openness to the possibility if not the probability that we're more than what we are, or think we are. "What no eye has seen, nor ear heard, nor the human heart conceived, what God has prepared for those who love him". . . (1 Cor. 2:9). Adventurousness, yes, but caution, too, and respect for the true rhythm of change as opposed to a feverish and precipitate grasping after newness. We're to be "wise as serpents and innocent as doves" (Mt. 10:16). We have to follow the evangelist's advice: "test the spirits" (1 Jn. 4:1). In following such dictates, whose example are we imitating if not that of the Son himself?

Returning to Jesus after getting to know 'Isa has been in a sense no problem at all because, of course, I never left him. Not that the credit for fidelity goes to me. Better to say that Jesus never left me.

The experience of getting to know 'Isa reminds me strongly of Mary Magdalene's moment in the garden when, after answering the angels, she turns around and sees Jesus standing there. But she fails to recognize him. So Jesus asks her:

"Woman, why are you weeping? Whom are you looking for?" Supposing him to be the gardener, she said to him, "Sir, if you have carried him away, tell me where you have laid him, and I will take him away." Jesus said to her, "Mary!" She turned and said to him in Hebrew, "Rabbouni!" (which means Teacher). (Jn. 20:15-16)

It isn't as simple as saying that 'Isa is like the gardener. It would be an injustice to Islam to claim that 'Isa is a kind of Jesus in disguise. And an injustice to Christianity to imply that the Son of God would only pretend to "empty himself." Rather whoever Jesus is—however we Christians agree that we can name *toward* him in our doctrine—he is not a prisoner of that doctrine. Nor of the images we make of him or of our expectations about how he looks or behaves, including our expectations about what it means for him to be "present" or "absent." It goes back to the freedom of God: the freedom to resist and escape from our possessiveness of him. "Do not hold onto me," Jesus tells Mary in the next verse in John, before telling her to go back to his brothers and tell them he is ascending.

Returning to Jesus from 'Isa also means being called to announce the Good News. Christ is indeed risen. In strange and unimaginable ways—in ways that defeat the understandings of Muslims and Christians alike. Nevertheless, our respective understandings point in a common direction, far off though the goal of true unity seems to lie. But God does not confuse unity with uniformity. Jesus is quite happy to have 'Isa as his ally in bringing all humanity home to God.

TEN ❧ *Tauhid* and *Trinity*

◆ The Odd Couple ◆

The "odd couple"—for that's the way my Muslim friend Aly Nahas described the two of us at the time—processed together down the aisle of St. Augustine Church in Rochester, NY, in January, 2004, at the beginning of Sunday Mass.

I'd agreed with him back then about our oddness. But I hadn't realized quite how odd we looked until I saw our images a few months later projected on a large video screen let down from the ceiling of the Conference Room at Rochester's Catholic Pastoral Center. There we paced, larger than life, the pink-faced Catholic Irishman, myself, and, marching beside me, the coffee-colored Muslim Egyptian, my friend, Aly. That we were both obviously on the far side of youth and even of middle-age was an element in common. So was the fact that Aly looked as comfortable with the gathering rite of the Mass as I or anyone else. But overriding any argument about similarity in age or behavior was the oddness of seeing us sharing in the celebration of the Mass together. We seemed to ooze oddness, to spread oddness all over each other and over everyone else as we processed towards the altar.

Aly's oddness was most obvious. It didn't take much imagination to ask what business a Muslim had marching in a procession like that. My own oddness was more subtle, more ambiguous. As a Catholic I had the right to walk in the procession, and as a Permanent Deacon I had the faculty to preach, as I'd been asked to do. But Aly had been asked not only to process in with me but to preach as well. We had in fact been asked to share the homily. Well then . . . What business did I have, a baptized and ordained person, sharing my right and faculty with someone who very obviously possessed neither? And what about the people gathered? What business did they have allowing this odd business to go forward? Didn't the oddness ooze over them, all the stickier the longer they let us get away with it?

Yet the people at that Mass had looked at us with friendly curiosity, not indignation. That was my impression at the time, one confirmed by glimpses of faces I caught in the screen's background as Aly and I entered camera range. Yet it wasn't Aly's and my good looks that had miraculously won people over and produced this effect. A lot of careful preparation by the pastoral staff at St. Augustine's had preceded Aly's and my visit. The front page of the church bulletin reproduced, in Arabic and in English translation, the *al-fatihah* or The Opening, the first sura or chapter of the Qur'an. Beneath that the staff had inserted a key sentence from the Agreement of Understanding and Cooperation between the Roman Catholic Diocese of Rochester and the Muslim Council of Masajid of Rochester, signed just that past May and still the only one of its kind in the country between a Catholic diocese and the local Muslim community. The sentence ran:

Affirming our faith in only one God, and recognizing our common history and shared Abrahamic traditions, we pray to the merciful God to inspire us in respect, mutual understanding, and love and to guide us to pursue our own common values for the benefit of our society and beyond.

Then the bulletin announced a connection between the Agreement and that Sunday's celebration of the Week of Prayer for Christian Unity, and asked parishioners to welcome Aly and me that morning as the first step taken in any local parish of our diocese to "honor and nurture this special relationship between our communities."

The parishioners could have been excused for thinking it a bit of a stretch to include Islam in a celebration of Christian Unity. Anticipating their skepticism, the pastor took pains before Mass began to invite people to "open their minds," as he put it, to the largest implications of the concept of Christian Unity. Christian Unity, he said, embraces unity with all creation. As for our Muslim sisters and brothers, they were not only members of that creation but also among the community of those who praised the one Creator. We Catholics had already acknowledged a common mission of praise with Muslims in the Agreement. So by including Islam in our understanding of unity that morning at Mass, we were just putting into action what we said in the Agreement itself: "Affirming our faith in only one God . . . we pray to the merciful God. . . ."

The editors of the video had inserted a bit of that pre-Mass talk, then had cut to the procession, then had made a further cut to the very beginning of my share of the homily. I got a little nervous at this point as I sat in the Conference Center months later watching events unfold on the large screen. I wondered how much the editors had decided to insert of what I'd said. The present occasion at the Pastoral Center didn't warrant long exposure. The video was being presented as background for a delicious dinner celebrating the first anniversary of the Agreement's signing. About a hundred people, a mixture of Catholics and Muslims, including our Bishop, Matthew Clark; the imam of the Islamic Center, Dr. Shafiq; and other signers of the original Agreement, were gathered in the Conference Center, and everyone was too busy enjoying the food to take in the fine and not-so-fine points of that particular Mass from back in January.

The editors had done their job well. They showed me explaining a little bit about the *sura al-fatihah*. I said that al-fatiha was very similar in length and content to the Lord's Prayer and that, like the Lord's Prayer, it had been given us by God to exemplify the way we should pray. I then read out loud from the pulpit the English translation:

> In the name of God, Most Gracious, Most Merciful,
> Praise be to God, the Cherisher and Sustainer of the
> Worlds;
> Most Gracious, Most Merciful;
> Master of the Day of Judgment.
> You do we worship, and your aid we seek.
> Show us the straight way,
> The way of those on whom you have bestowed your
> favor, those whose portion is not wrath, and who go
> not astray.
> Amen.

The video editors cut out what followed, my recitation of al-fatihah in Arabic. They cut out my homily too.

My vanity cried out within me in indignation at the cuts. Good sense won the day, however. My accent in Arabic falls somewhat short of perfection, as Aly always takes great delight in reminding me. In fact, we'd bantered about my bad accent at all three Masses that Sunday. But the banter was edited out also, and Aly's share of the homily—a quick presentation of the main tenets of Islam—was cut down to a small sample. The blow to his ego (assuming that he felt it—I didn't ask him) was as great as to mine. I took some consolation from that.

Preserved in its entirety, though, was the most inspired moment of that particular Mass. Neither Aly nor I could claim credit for it. Instead, the pastor and presider, a priest noted for his creativity in constructing symbols of unity binding diverse populations, was inspiration's vehicle.

It happened like this. The videotaped version we were watching that evening at the Conference Center was actually the third of the three Masses Aly and I had taken part in that Sunday. The pastor had presided over the second of them and had obviously been thinking since then about ways of knitting Aly's and my particular contributions more tightly into the fabric of the celebration. So when it came time for that third and final Mass, he was ready. I don't recall that he disclosed his intention to us before the Mass began. What I remember is my surprise and delight at hearing him say boldly and confidently to the congregation, just before the kiss of peace, when we Catholics normally recite the Lord's Prayer, that we would this time all join hands and recite instead the translation of the Fatiha printed in the bulletin. And that's what people did, as smoothly as if they'd been doing it all their lives. Months later, at the Conference Center, the busy diners all put down their forks in order to watch this event on the big screen. The video camera panned across the Catholic congregation, itself a mixture of races and ethnicities as, in unison, each person recited al-fatiha, and with conviction, as if this prayer "counted" as much as the one we normally say.

And doesn't it? True, God is not addressed in al-fatihah as "Father," and there is no direct reference to God's forgiving our sins in the measure in which we forgive others'. But to call God "most gracious" and "most merciful" is to name the same God, or at least name *toward* the same God, to whom we Christians appeal in the Lord's Prayer. For it is to the God that we Christians and Muslims both appeal, to the one and only God who "cherishes and sustains" the worlds. This God, majestic as he may be, nevertheless condescends to offer us human creatures guidance. And he provides us with a model prayer in which we can ask for that guidance and give praise for receiving it, at the same time as he reminds us that it is possible for us to go astray (compare "lead us not unto temptation"), that the consequences of going astray are drastic, and that he awaits us at Judgment Day to reward us according to whether we've stayed on or strayed from that path.

In short, nothing in al-fatihah seems to present an obvious stumbling block to Christians seeking to address the one God in the spirit of the Lord's Prayer. This was the conclusion apparently reached, first by the pastor and then affirmed by the members of the congregation in church that day. If *lex orandi, lex credendi* is true (if the rule of prayer determines the rule of belief, and not vice versa), then a tiny but significant step in the history of faith was taken that Sunday morning in January. The Mass at St. Augustine's proved that it really is possible for Christians to pray as Muslims pray, because what matters above all else is a desire to praise God as one family of believers.

It matters to God because it was one humanity that he created. It matters to us because of our tendency to split humanity into pieces and to rank some of those pieces (especially our own piece) higher on the scale of creation than others.

Yet the desire to praise God together doesn't lead to a blending of one religion with the other. That's because Aly and I, and the Islam and the Christianity we represented during that Mass, really were and are an "odd couple." We didn't and don't fit together. Nothing either of us had said, or that the presider had said, denied that oddness. And yet superseding the oddness was the greater fittedness: that our common orientation in prayer toward the one God revealed our deepest similarity. Aly and I might not fit with each other, but we fit with God, and the rest of the congregation fit with God along with us, as did those diners at the Pastoral Center looking on later, in a oneness of desire that brought "Our Father" and "Cherisher and Sustainer" into common focus as the One and Only God.

The *Tauhid* of God was revealed in the Tauhid of the desire to praise him.

◆ One or Three? ◆

Tauhid is the word that asserts Islam's monotheism, the fundamental belief that God is One. So the Tauhid cherished by Muslims would ordinarily resist such focus, such sharing of place with a concept—that of the Trinity—which the Qur'an explicitly regards as "odd" in the negative sense, and even as aberrant:

For indeed they disbelieve who say, "God is three of three" [i.e., in a trinity], when the truth is there is no god but One

God. And if they do not restrain themselves from saying these things, there will fall on those of them who disbelieve a terrible punishment. (*sura al-ma'idah* 5:73)

The vehemence of the Qur'anic utterance and its unmistakable reference to Christian belief (at least to those churches that honor the Nicene Creed, in which Trinitarian belief is proclaimed) seems to leave little room for the kind of Tauhid manifested at the Mass for Christian Unity at St. Augustine's. If the Christians at that Mass had also seen this passage from the Qur'an printed on their bulletins, would they have been so willing to join in on al-fatihah, in substitution for the Lord's Prayer? And as for Muslims . . . I didn't ask Aly what he was thinking when he stood in the altar area listening to the congregation recite the Nicene Creed. Could he even have recited the Creed's first line—"We believe in one God, the father almighty, maker of heaven and earth . . ."? There's no question that he would have had to reject the second line, "And in Jesus Christ, his only Son. . . ." But to call God "father" presupposes an intimacy or familiarity in Christians' imagining of God that jars with Muslims' explicit sense of God's awesome dignity.

So it seems that the desire for Muslim and Christian unity in praise expressed during the Mass at St. Augustine's might stand on shakier ground than we thought. Can anything save it?

Looking more carefully at the Qur'an's objection to the concept of the Trinity, we might argue that the objection is based on a mere misunderstanding. In the verse above, for example—and it is a typical formulation of the Muslim objection—what the Qur'an appears to deny is a concept of tri-theism. As if when we Christians pray in the name of Father, Son, and Holy Spirit, we are praying to three separate gods. Well, we Christians would object to such a notion as much as Muslims do!

The actual naming of the persons of the Trinity is also based on a misunderstanding—and so seems equally capable of easy correction. The mis-naming occurs in several places. One of them is in a passage already mentioned in Chapter Four where God is interrogating 'Isa on the Day of Judgment:

> And behold! God will say on that day: "O 'Isa, son of Mary, did you ever say to humankind, 'Take me and my mother as gods in addition to God? . . ." (*sura al-ma'idah* 5:116)

Again, we Christians would find a naming of the Trinity as Father, Son, and Mary just as problematic as Muslims do. So the question naturally arises: Why can't we Christians and Muslims just sit down like reasonable people and clear up these misconceptions once for all? Doesn't the need to find some common ground for our praise of the God whom we all claim is the same God and the only true God override such slips and absurdities?

Alas, it's not that easy. The hope of justifying a desire for unity of worship vanishes the minute we absorb the fact that in the verse above, God is objecting not simply to a naming of Mary as a member of the Godhead, but to any association whatever of a mortal human being with himself, including any association with 'Isa. It's not that the Qur'an has got the Trinity "wrong"; the Qur'an is acting very consistently according to its understanding of who 'Isa is. We recall, from our discussion in the previous chapter, that 'Isa is no more (but no less) than a prophet. On that basis, the Qur'an is quite right to reject both Mary's and 'Isa's inclusion in the Godhead. Wouldn't we Christians have to do the same?

To revisit briefly a point made in the previous chapter, it's hard not to admire 'Isa (however grudgingly) when, in the next section of the verse printed just above, he replies in self-defense to God's interrogation at Judgment Day:

Glory be to you! Never would I say what I have no right to say. If I had, you would have known it. You know what is in my heart. I do not know what is in yours. For indeed you know all hidden things.

'Isa speaks truly. He never did claim to be more than an 'abd, a servant. And yet, and yet . . . there couldn't be a more explicit contradiction between what 'Isa has just said to God and what Jesus says to God in John 17:22-23:

"The glory you have given me I have given them [i.e., the disciples] so that they may be one, as we are one, I in them, you in me, that they may become completely one."

'Isa or Jesus? Muslims claim that in Jesus we've turned a suitably humble prophet into God's equal. The incompatibility between Tauhid and Trinity follows from this mistaking of divine and human identity.

That's not all that follows. The Qur'anic rejection of the Trinity includes a rejection not only of a divinized 'Isa, but also of humankind's place within the Trinitarian relationship, as "adopted sons and daughters," in Paul's vocabulary, or, in John's, as "friends." According to the Qur'an, absolutely nothing, not any other god (assuming even for the sake of argument that there could exist such a thing as a rival to God!), and certainly not any human being, not even God's own greatest prophets, like Abraham or Moses or 'Isa, not even the prophet Muhammad himself, can share in any part of what is God. Tauhid is jealously guarded in the Qur'an because it maintains the necessary boundary between what belongs to God and what belongs to us. In Christianity, by contrast, "unity" is what God, through the Holy Spirit, actively and lovingly invites us in Jesus Christ to share.

Or as the Qur'an puts it in many places, and as Muslims confess it in the Shahadah or confession, one of the Five Pillars: "There is no god but God." In the Qur'an, God is merciful and cares for humankind, but the relationship between God and his creation is fundamentally and absolutely asymmetric. God is indeed "odd": singular, self-sufficient, whole, indivisible, all-powerful. His human creation doesn't simply manifest the opposite of these and other divine attributes, for "opposite" implies the two orders are comparable. We are his 'abad or servants, created for praising him and for receiving the rewards of that praise in the life to come. But those rewards do not, could not, include sharing in the divine life.

"Do not, could not . . ." Is what I've said true? Should I put the difference between rival conceptions of God so starkly? From just the Qur'anic verses cited above, we get an inkling of what happens with the concept of Tauhid throughout the Qur'an, that it is a concept formulated in and through polemics. Exaggeration tends to affect its expression. This isn't to suggest that the Qur'an doesn't mean what it says about God as One. What it does suggest is that we need to understand the historical context in which the Qur'an says it.

That context is complex. Muhammad's relationships with Christians were ambiguous. In some verses, the Qur'an speaks very warmly about certain Christians, especially monks, and their openness to the revelations that Muhammad received. Christian monks were said to have encouraged Muhammad during the first years of his ministry, when he was uncertain about whether the divine "auditions" he was receiving were authentic or not. The Christian *negus* or king of Abyssinia received kindly the group of Muhammad's followers who in the early days of Islam emigrated to that country in order to escape persecution in Mecca (this emigration is often referred to as the first hijrah, Muhammad's later and far more consequential emigration to Yathrib, later renamed Medina, being the second). But other Christians seem to have resisted the revelations, or certain parts of them—most probably those parts that characterize Jesus as 'Isa the prophet and no more. Verses like the ones about 'Isa discussed above may have been prompted and sharpened by such resistance.

But it wasn't Christians with their Trinitarianism who mounted the stiffest challenge to Tauhid. It was the paganism of the Arab tribes, and especially of Muhammad's own Quraish clan in Mecca, which forced the language of Tauhid into a polemical mold. The revelations Muhammad was receiving from the one God declared, without equivocation, that the gods worshiped by the Quraish and the other Arab tribes were nothing—as were the human behaviors demanded by those illusory deities: proud self-reliance, indifference to social inferiors, implacable hostility to the members of other tribes (and to their gods). The Quraish fought back, recognizing in these revelations a fundamental challenge not only to their own prized cultic practices but also to the income they received from hosting the annual Hajj or pilgrimage to Mecca. During a brief period of truce each year the other tribes would journey to Mecca to worship at the Ka'bah where idols of their deities were housed. Tauhid threatened the underpinnings of polytheistic cultic and social reality.

But the Qur'an's critique of paganism, and its consequent emphasis on the absoluteness of Tauhid, goes even deeper. In verse after verse the point is hammered home that the worship of idols isn't simply a special problem to be combated among ignorant Bedouin tribesmen of the Arabic peninsula. It is a fundamental human temptation. At issue is egoism: the human craving for self-sufficiency. Worship of false gods is ultimately worship of ourselves. The attraction of self-worship is like a drug that befuddles the intellect, dulls the memory, casts a shroud over the senses, and leaves us prey to obsession. All of us, in all times and places, are vulnerable to it.

Monotheists are not exempt from the temptation—hence the Qur'an's criticism of Jews and Christians, as well as of Muslims themselves, who are repeatedly warned not to become complacent about their Tauhid. In fact, the Tauhid of monotheists is exposed to an evil from which polytheists are exempt: hypocrisy.

> But when the hypocrites meet those who believe, they say, "We believe!" But when they are alone with their satans [i.e., with their obsessions, for wealth, prestige, etc.], they say, "We're really on your side! Before, we were only fooling!" Well, God will turn the fooling back on them! He will let them indulge their transgressions for a while as they go wandering in a maze. (*sura al-bakarah* 2:14-15)

It could be said that the main ethical weight of the Qur'an, in its negative moment, lies right here: in the relentless effort to warn believers themselves of the danger of falling away from

Tauhid into self-destructive obsessiveness—an obsessiveness that always seeks its own little idol to worship under cover of allegiance to God.

Given the Qur'anic urgency to dispel the human fascination with what the Qur'an calls shirk or the associating of idols with God, it's not surprising that God is proclaimed to be inviolable in his awesome majesty. Yet this Tauhid does not, as we might expect, result in a God who is hard, cold, remote, aloof. Nor does God demand servility on the part of "mere" mortals. The 'abad of God are not slaves of God but willing servants. Islam is better translated self-surrender than submission. And the physical gesture of prayer, sujud, which expresses this islam, is better seen as a profound bow of humility than as prostration. God is "most gracious, most merciful"—to cite the characteristics of God most frequently cited by Muslims themselves. God is most concerned that we live together now in peace, but not as an end in itself. God's main focus (if I may put it that way) is on our living in peace now so that we may enjoy the fruits of true peace in the life to come.

What that life to come will be like is painted in greater detail in the Qur'an than in our own Scripture. The life to come is described in many places in the Qur'an as a great banquet. The talk at that table among God's 'abad will be about salaam or peace. But God himself will join the company to tie up some loose ends. Here's how one Qur'anic verse describes the divine table-talk:

To each of you Jews, Christians, Muslims we have given a rule and a clear pattern. If God had wanted, he could have made you one ummah or community. But he chose rather to test you in those gifts he has given you. So compete with each other in doing good works. To God you shall all return.

At that time we will make clear to you all those matters about which you are now disputing. (*sura al-ma'idah* 5:48)

These verses are not without irony. For all the polemics about Tauhid and other topics of theological dispute among the tribes and the religions, what really matters is that we praise God and serve each other. The final word about whether God is one or three or both will have to wait until that heavenly banquet when the answer will be seated right in front of us.

◆ To the Trinity by Way of Tauhid ◆

Returning from Tauhid to the Trinity, we're made newly aware of an old truth: that while the issue of God's oneness has been tragically divisive for all the religions of Abraham, it has at the same time been powerfully productive, at least for Christianity and Islam (leaving aside what the issue has meant for Judaism). I speak of the ongoing richness of trinitarian thought and of the continuing ethical freshness and bracingness of Tauhid as articulated in the Qur'an.

As for the tragic divisiveness of the issue of God's oneness, the Gospel itself is the best source.

When Jesus stands before the high priest in Mark 14:61–64, he is asked:

"Are you the Messiah, the Son of the Blessed One?" Jesus said, "I am; and 'you will see the Son of Man seated at the right hand of the Power,' and 'coming with the clouds of heaven.'" Then the high priest tore his clothes and said, "Why do we still need witnesses? You have heard his blasphemy!"

Whatever the other and more decisive motives behind the chief priest's and the elders condemnation of Jesus (fear of the Romans, fear of losing their authority among the Jewish populace), not to be discounted is this almost visceral rejection of any mortal being's claim to be "Son of the Blessed One." God is God. Humans are humans. There is a deep and understandable resistance within all of us to any apparent confounding of the two. Judaism continues to maintain this resistance. And so, of course, does Islam.

The Muslim version of this fundamental resistance occurs in *al-ikhlas* or "Purity," the sura often cited as the pre-eminent statement of Tauhid:

> Say: "He, God, is One.
> God is eternal, self-sufficient.
> He does not beget offspring, nor was he begotten.
> To him there is absolutely nothing comparable."

Again, there's no use protesting that this very strongly implied critique of Jesus' sonship is based on a misunderstanding, as if Christians ever thought that Jesus was a son in the literal sense or that for God to have a son compromises God's power and independence (by suggesting that God, like a worn-out CEO, couldn't do all God's work without a son's assistance). We have to face the fact that, for the Qur'an, all language, no matter how sophisticated, that differentiates or "associates" God with any other created being is inadmissible.

Presumably St. Paul, in an earlier century, is referring to the challenge posed by such resistance when he says:

> Jews demand signs and Greeks desire wisdom, but we proclaim Christ crucified, a stumbling block to Jews and foolishness to Gentiles. . . . (1 Cor. 1:22)

Stumbling block and foolishness both: A God whose Son dies a mortal's death, and the most shameful of deaths, on a Roman cross, and then is (supposedly) resurrected into new life in God!

St. Paul didn't draw the explicit conclusion reached later at the Ecumenical Councils, that the One God is Father, Son, and Spirit. But returning from Tauhid to the Trinity reminds us that this very conclusion resulted from difficulties Christians themselves had in knowing how far they, and we, should push the idea of sonship. Shouldn't "wisdom" restrain us after all? The Arian heresy of the fourth century was based on the eminently logical notion—echoed three centuries later in *sura al-ikhlas*—that a truly self-sufficient God would never produce a "son." As a result, "son" had to be used in a derivative, honorific sense, of Jesus Christ as a being supremely endowed with prestige and power but nevertheless a creature. True, the Council of Nicea (325 CE) rejected Arius's seeming reasonableness. Yet the controversy did not stop. For a while, bishops favorable to Arius prevailed against the Nicean trinitarian formulation.

Subsequent ecumenical councils, especially the Councils of Constantinople in 385 CE and of Chalcedon in 451 CE, were necessary in order to establish unequivocally that God was Three in One. "Unequivocally" isn't the right word, however. The Councils produced the ground rules for all subsequent Christian discourse on God: that the one God is three Persons. But the ground rules were never intended to take the place of the game. The power of these early formulations is that they have allowed for the rich development of Trinitarian discussion throughout the centuries. A discussion that is as exciting and vital now as it has ever been.

Returning from Tauhid to the Trinity challenges us to review this discussion with new seriousness. Tauhid has vigorously opposed the very basis of it. Well, then, rather than react defensively and barricade ourselves within a credal formulation we only dimly understand, what we ought to do is reexamine Trinitarianism for ourselves. What do we really mean when we say we believe in God the Father, in Christ the Son, and in the Holy Spirit? Are we closet tri-theists after all? Or closet modalists (believing that Father, Son, and Spirit are merely modes or phases in the saving action of God)? Or closet monophysites (believing that Jesus Christ is a strictly spiritual being who once put on humanity like a suit of filthy old clothes, shucking them when done with them)? Or even closet Arians? Or any one of a number of other Trinitarians who fail to play by the ground rules?

Alas, though, the spirit is willing, but the flesh. . . . We run to our nearest theological library to help us get answers to our questions. We zealously collect the necessary books, but one glance inside those tomes is all it will probably take to make most of us weak in the knees. Trinitarian theology is not light reading! But the best of it is not impossible, nor trivial. Or if one or other representative of it proves to be so, then it truly does fall under Tauhid's critique, for representing a supremely dangerous misuse of the intellect. And even worse: for possibly being idolatrous as well, substituting a mere intellectual exercise for a deeply prayerful search into the ways of a God who truly sent himself in his Son to live among us and raise us to the God-life through his Holy Spirit.

That same search has to develop a longer reach. It is no longer enough for Trinitarianism to contain itself within Christianity, as if valid only there. Catholic Christians since Vatican II have agreed that if God in Jesus through the Holy Spirit saves, this same God saves everyone, and that includes Muslims. Yet this longer Trinitarian reach can't just be assumed to fold Islam (or any other religion) neatly in its embrace. It can't simply turn Muslims (or Jews and Buddhists) into "anonymous Christians" through a Holy Spirit who transforms them without their even knowing it. Trinitarianism can't be used mechanically, like a hat that must fit every head. On the contrary, a healthy Trinitarianism searches for language that can respect a variety of understandings of God, even an understanding like Tauhid's which stands in vigorous opposition to Trinitarianism's own.

We Christians don't lack for contemporary examples of healthy—and readable!—Trinitarianism. S. Mark Heim, for example, in *The Depths of the Riches: A Trinitarian Theology of Religious Ends*, clearly and cogently argues that by looking at what each of the major religions believes to be its end or goal, we avoid sterile stalemate over competing understandings of God. Christianity envisions salvation as its end. Understood as restoration to relationship with God, salvation is made possible by a God who is himself a relationship of persons. For Muslims, the religious end is relational too, though primarily with God's creation rather than with God himself, who stands above that creation as its sole source and monitor. Salvation (as Christians understand it) is not at issue for Muslims. Salaam is. Yet each of these ends, while different, contains elements of the other. Christians can recognize elements of salaam in the kingdom of heaven. Muslims can recognize elements of salvation in the *fana'* or self-forgetfulness of Sufi mystical union with God. Nothing forces either Muslims or Christians to believe that the same God could not have willed either the differences or the congruencies of Christian and Muslim ends.

Trinitarianism and Tauhid really do well to march along together towards their respective goals—salvation for the one, salaam for the other—as an "odd couple." Not only theologians but the great majority of the inhabitants of our planet long for them to do so. Better an "odd couple" than adversaries with hands locked around each other's throats. But the simple opposite to a hostile relationship isn't desirable either. Trinitarianism and Tauhid will strengthen each other not by embarrassed attempts by Muslims and Christians either to ignore differences or to blend them. Trinitarianism and Tauhid will strengthen each other as Muslims and Christians get used to each other's differences. Honestly naming those differences. Honestly naming congruences also. Seeing the differences and congruences as signs of God's favor. Competing in one sphere only, in doing good works.

And then, finally, delighting in the heavenly banquet where the Keynote Speaker will put all oddness to rest at last, except the oddness of the number One.

ELEVEN Hijab *and the* Veil of the Temple

◆ Muslim Women and the Hijab ◆

At first glance, nothing could seem more clearly a sign of difference between Christianity and Islam than the Hijab. After all, a Hijab is a scarf covering the heads of Muslim women. A light piece of fabric. How does it stretch to cover the differences between the religions themselves?

For me, the stretching began early, in the Walt Disney comic books I doted on as a child. Donald Duck and Uncle Scrooge, along with Donald's intrepid nephews, Huey, Dewey, and Louie, were my initial guides into Islam. In the Ducks' version of the fabled land of the Mysterious East, the cartoon panels no longer contained cars on brown roads but rather camels on yellow sand. No longer generic bulbs of green on brown sticks but curved palm trees. No longer escaped convicts in stripes but assassins brandishing scimitars. No longer Daisy Duck in bow and apron but silent statues in harem pants following the movements of the intruding Ducks from the corners of their raccoon-like eyes, the rest of their faces covered by pink or lavender gauze. My first glimpse of the Hijab.

The relatively innocent image of the Hijab that I absorbed as a child from Walt Disney grew more profane over the years—I'm thinking now of belly-dancers waving their transparent Hijabs at fat, lascivious sultans: images that would make their way into cheap novels and bad movies. Early or late the Hijab was never more than a symbol of the ambiguous otherness of Islam: both forbidden and enticingly offered, both chilling and provoking at the same time.

I don't recall ever being in the same room with real flesh-and-blood Muslim women wearing Hijabs until I started to take Arabic lessons at the Islamic Center. These women still seemed mysterious, but in a more profound way. These women were not culturally created screens upon which I was invited to project my pre- and post-pubescent fantasies of adventure. These women were human beings, intelligent ones, determined to place the screen of the Hijab between themselves and those very fantasies of mine and of any other male not in their family.

After I'd been at the Islamic Center for a year or so and had gotten well into the study of the Qur'an with Omar, I began bringing my high school English students to the Center to observe Friday prayers (when the whole local ummah is assembled) and afterward to meet with and ask questions about Islam of the members of the Center. This is when I began actually to talk with Muslim women, for they were as ready and able as the men to explain their faith and its practices both to me and to my students.

A lot of the questions the students asked were about the Hijab. Even more were about why Muslim men and women worshiped separately, in different spaces. (In Rochester's Islamic Center, the men do Salat or public prayer in the large main worship space on the ground floor. Women gather in the balcony in back, overlooking the men's area.)

The Muslim women who spoke up at that point did so articulately and with great vigor. None of them remotely resembled the most recent kind of image I had projected upon Muslim women prior to coming to the Center, that of broken-spirited victims of male domination. The women at the Center asserted in no uncertain terms that both the Hijab and the separation for prayer served the same function: that of denying men (or the "weaker sex," as the women put it, with slightly condescending smiles) the excuse of sexual attraction to justify men's failure to live up to their Islam or total self-giving to God. Women gathered for prayer separately in a space behind the men because women wouldn't be distracted as men would be if they were the ones gathered behind the women during the bodily movement of sujud or bowing down to the ground. And if we wanted to follow the symbolism rigorously, the women advised us, we'd see that by their gathering in an area overlooking and above the men, Muslim women were sending a message about who the real boss was.

The women's handling of questions about the Hijab followed the same line. The Hijab, like the physical separation of men and women at Salat or daily prayer, far from being a sign of male oppression, was actually a sign of the opposite: of resistance to such oppression. The Hijab, along with the qameez (the loose-fitting tunic), the shalwar (the flowing ankle-length skirt), and the *jilbab* (the full-length gown often worn over both qameez and shalwar)—these garments fulfilled for women the Qur'anic decree that both sexes should dress modestly so as not to create stumbling blocks for each other. If obedience to the decree seemed more strikingly evident in women's dress than in men's, that was because of the Western penchant for turning women into blatant sexual objects, in fashions, advertisements, movies,

TV, and everywhere else. What a scandal! Didn't Western women have any respect for themselves? Why did they allow themselves to become shaped by men's fantasies in this way!

The Muslim women didn't want to embarrass my students, so they didn't say any more than necessary about Western sexual exploitation. But they said enough to get the boys and especially the girls thinking, not so much about Islam, as about why it was that "modesty" in dress and behavior had become such a scorned value in American mainstream culture, to which almost all of my students belonged.

I myself was aware even at that time that the Hijab and the separation of men and women in Islam had a more complex meaning than the women at the Islamic Center were giving it. And that a large part of this meaning had been made by Westerners, as evidenced even in the adventures of Donald Duck. But I didn't put our hosts at the Islamic Center on the spot by demanding there and then a fuller account. It seemed clear to me that the women at the Center were competing for control over the Hijab as symbol. I, for one, wished them well. If anyone should have ownership of the Hijab, the women of Islam should be the ones: not Muslim men, and certainly not non-Muslims of either sex.

Yet symbols are hard to tame. Try to keep one for a pet and you'll have a battle on your hands!

The Hijab could even raise an argument among "liberated" Muslim women. I found that out at an Islamic conference I attended some time later. One of the speakers there, a white female convert to Islam from Christianity, addressed the topic of "Women's Activism in Islam" by arguing that Islam has always been reformist if not revolutionary at heart and that this central theme is nowhere more evident than in the Qur'an's assertion of women's equality with men. Muhammad's relationships with women, and especially with his wives, the speaker asserted, bear out this fundamental understanding of women's equal place, as does the subsequent historical record of female leadership in Muslim-controlled lands. Misogynist cultural influences—similar to those that influenced a parallel misogynist development in Christianity—explain the lamentable locking-up of Muslim women in enforced seclusion, where the Hijab became a sign of enslavement. Yet (the speaker concluded) the Hijab actually represented a key element of the liberating essence of true Islam. It did so not only by reinforcing self-respect for both women and men (by diminishing the force of mere physical attractiveness in healthy self-images and relationships), but also by reminding Muslims that Islam means a surrender to God's will, not to their own. Muslim women were privileged to bear this sign of self-surrendering in such an unmistakable way. Women were uniquely gifted to display before the whole world and to each other the badge of all Muslims' special commitment to God.

All of this sounded fine in the abstract, but I wasn't so sure that the symbolic messiness of the Hijab could be ironed out so easily. I was much more aware by this time of how deeply the Western colonialization of Muslim lands since the beginning of the nineteenth century had affected Muslims' own understanding of the Hijab. For most Westerners, the Hijab came to represent all that seemed retrograde about Islam: its cultural "backwardness" as well as its "oriental" prurience (the sultans, the dancing girls, etc.), in contrast to the God-given superiority of Christianity and Western culture and moral values generally. This superiority was manifested primarily in military might and technological know-how, but also—so went the propaganda of the time—in political organization, moral strictness, and respect for women's rights. Yet Western males otherwise hostile to feminists and suffragettes in their own countries saw no contradiction in pointing to the Hijab as evidence of Muslim decadence and contempt for the "fair sex." Muslims, both male and female, reacted defensively to this attack. They gave the Hijab new value as a sign of what distinguished Islam from the dominating culture of the West. Many Muslim women began to wear the Hijab in proud protest against the Western critique. At least some women did.

This brings me back to the speaker at the conference I attended. The speaker was one of those Muslim women who wore her own Hijab and the other traditional garments proudly—as I would have expected her to do, given the thrust of her speech. What surprised me, though, was the passionate scorn she had for immigrant Muslim women she'd met here in the U.S. who had cast off their Hijabs with relief as soon as they'd reached our shores. Had they no respect for themselves and for Islam? As the speaker went on in this vein, I looked at the audience around me. All the Muslim women in attendance seemed to be wearing the Hijab. So presumably they were feeling confirmed in their way of presenting themselves to others, both to Muslims and non-Muslims. To fellow Muslims, their wearing the Hijab asserted their solidarity. To non-Muslims, their wearing the Hijab asserted their difference.

But no: these weren't the only Muslim women present. On the other side of the auditorium from where I was sitting, I spotted two women, Muslim friends of mine, both immigrants, who were not only not wearing the Hijab; they were wearing Western clothing—modestly conservative in color and cut, to be sure, but emphatically not "Muslim." How were they feeling,

I wondered, as the speaker's diatribe went on against those who had abandoned the veil?

I spotted those women at the conference luncheon afterward and went over to sit with them. While chatting about this and that, I kept wondering whether I should ask my two friends about their reaction to the speaker's vehemence. I didn't see how they could not have felt uncomfortable. Would I make them feel doubly uncomfortable by calling attention to their supposed discomfort? What right did I have, a non-Muslim, and a male, to pry into private matters? If I did ask the women about their reaction, how could I expect them to be candid with me?

Then, and not for the last time, curiosity overcame discretion. I blurted out my question. Without hesitating both women replied, "Oh, no, we weren't uncomfortable. Wearing or not wearing the veil is a matter of choice. Except at the mosque, of course." I wasn't bold enough to press further by asking, "Choice between what, exactly?" though I wish I had been. After all, my friends didn't seem in any way to have been offended or even embarrassed by my raising the issue of the Hijab. And yet I felt I'd been gently put in my place. Whatever discomfort my friends might have felt at the speaker's vehemence remained hidden, veiled behind a metaphorical Hijab, as it were: in any case off-limits to a non-Muslim male. I tried to accept my exclusion graciously.

One lesson from the speaker's talk and the conversations afterwards seemed clear: The Hijab is a powerful sign of difference whether or not a Muslim woman actually wears it. By wearing it she is different not only from non-Muslim women but from Muslim women who don't wear it—though the difference in this instance is a different difference! And by not wearing it, except when praying Salat, she is obviously different from

Muslim women who do. But is this difference enough to make her indistinguishable from non-Muslim women? My friends would have said no. The speaker would probably have said yes. She might also have said that the indistinguishableness implies a kind of betrayal or apostasy. The Hijab seems caught in a tug-of-war between those Muslim women who want it to carry the sign of difference out into the non-Muslim world, and those Muslim women who want it to operate only in the context of worship. Clearly the struggle owes some of its passion to unresolved tensions between immigrant Muslim women eager to throw off a symbol of male oppression (which the Hijab can be in certain countries) and American converts, like the speaker at the conference, anxious to assert their new identity in a multicultural context. Whatever the sources of the struggle, however, it is being played out in a civil society here in the U.S. which does not force a particular choice on Muslim women. The women are left to make their own choices, to work out the meaning of the symbol for themselves.

I like the way this freedom is being exercised in the American setting—or at least I like the way it is being exercised in Rochester. Cultural diversity among Muslims at the Islamic Center contributes to my growing sense of the Hijab and the qameez, shalwar, and jilbab as celebratory garments. African women wrap themselves head to toe in brightly colored materials. Women from other Muslim countries wear garments ranging from dark and sober to light and festive. The variety is striking, as expressive both of a range of cultural norms and of personal choices. Personal choices which often proceed from a deep spirituality.

My friend Yasmin, in her own handling of the Hijab and the other garments, embodies this spiritually grounded freedom vividly. Yasmin is truly Muslim in that inward and public piety are vigorously and creatively combined and mutually sustaining. (I think of the desired Muslim unity of 'Abd and Wali, servant and saint.) A devoted mother and wife, she is a tireless volunteer at the Center, offering herself for any number of challenging projects, from founding and directing an Islamic school, to arranging conferences, to speaking about Islam publicly. (I described, in the Jihad chapter, just one of many instances where she has spoken up bravely in defense of her community's rights.) Yasmin is also—as if she weren't busy or talented enough—a professor of clinical chemistry.

The reason I'm mentioning Yasmin in the context of a discussion of the public and spiritual meaning of the Hijab is that she is also a dress designer of great talent, designing and making her own Hijabs and qameezes, shalwars, and jilbabs. Beautiful in texture and color, these garments do not call attention to the wearer the way Western clothing tends to do. I call Yasmin's Hijabs and other garments spiritual because they call attention to the *ihsan* or beauty of Islam, Islam in its highest form, as total self-giving to God in salaam or peace. As the hadith or story based on Muhammad's encounter with an angelic white-haired stranger says: "Pray to God as if you could see him, or if you cannot, pray knowing that he can see you." The folds of shades of yellow and gold cloth both obscuring and revealing hand-painted panels, or the sometimes subtler shades of lavender and magenta, flowing or gathered—all express the spirituality of delighted presence. In much the same way that Muslim art is based on the joyful extensions and transformations of Arabic script into calligraphy and into design both pictorial and architectural, Yasmin's artistry with the Hijab extends and transforms the traditional garment into a symbol of praise.

Difference from non-Muslims is still asserted. But because the symbol, thanks to the beauty of fabric, color, and design, opens primarily to God, rather than exclusively within a closed network of intra-religious and intra-cultural meanings, the Hijab and the other garments, as Yasmin has shaped them, invite all of us to find and to express that same center of transforming joy within ourselves and our own faith traditions.

◆ The Many Meanings of Hijab ◆

It is wonderful to see a drab Arabic word take on rich coloring both in the Qur'an and in Islam's subsequent history, like plain fabric transformed by Yasmin's hands.

Hijab in its verbal form simply means "cover, shut from view." *Hijab* as a noun refers to any physical object that veils or curtains anything else. A door could be a hijab. A wall.

Hijab is used only seven times in the Qur'an. So the current importance of the term far exceeds its importance in Muslim scripture itself. But that doesn't mean that the subsequent increase in importance isn't itself important, or that those earliest appearances of the term don't hold important clues for our present understanding. Let's look at how the term has increased in substance to cover all of us in its folds, Muslim and Christian alike.

The term was expandable right from the beginning. Of those seven occurrences in the Qur'an, Hijab means "face veil" in only one of them, and even there the full meaning was developed later on, in subsequent interpretation.

The "occasion of revelation" (the Muslim phrase for a specific historical event that called forth a particular Qur'anic ayah or verse) was no more and no less than the rowdiness of certain wedding guests.

According to *hadith* and other traditional accounts, prophet Muhammad's lodgings at Medina quickly became a general gathering place for the ummah. His apartments, and those of his wives, directly adjoined the simple prayer area. People came and went freely, both men and women, and access to the prophet was nearly always available.

The ummah's rapid growth affected that easy family-style commerce. The prophet's patience was tried again and again, particularly by invasions of his wives' space. Finally came the last straw. The story goes that guests overstayed their welcome at the celebration of Muhammad's marriage to Zaynab bint Jahsh. One of them, Muhammad's own servant, was so importuning that Muhammad had to set up a barrier, a curtain (hijab), to prevent the fellow from barging into Zaynab's chamber. The situation was serious enough to warrant the following verse:

And when any of you ask Muhammad's wives for household things, ask for them from behind a screen [hijab]. This will make relations purer and more proper, both for you and for them. (*sura al-ahzab* 33.53)

Subsequent ayat or verses reinforce the need to protect family space. From these it is apparent that the need arose not just from the importunings of one boorish wedding guest but also from the malevolence of munafiqun or hypocrites seeking to undermine prophet Muhammad's authority by treating his wives with contempt. The Qur'an's stern injunction against "annoying" the Prophet (at 33:53, but also at 33:57 and 58) points out the way that an excess of hospitality could open the gate to sedition. There had to be a limit, there had to be a difference, there had to be protection of prophet Muhammad's privacy and dignity, protection marked, in the first instance, by simple courtesy.

So Hijab enters world history as a divine expedient to help Muhammad cope with the downside of success: with the boisterousness of true followers and the malice of the envious. Hijab at this point does not refer to the face veil but to a barrier or curtain set up at the doors of all Muhammad's wives quarters to protect their privacy and ensure respect.

The momentous subsequent history of the Hijab is a story well told by contemporary Muslim feminists like Leila Ahmed, Fatima Mernisi, Amina Wadud and others: the Hijab's transformation from a means of protecting Muhammad's wives' private space to a face veil protecting his wives' persons when they ventured outside the family compound, from an obligatory garment screening not only Muhammad's wives but all women of the young ummah to the total seclusion of Muslim women during the Abbasid caliphate in Iraq. The story is told against the backdrop of a recovered Qur'anic egalitarianism. Much of what comes to light in such tellings is the role cultural influences played in the post-Qur'anic development of the Hijab as a negative symbol of women's suppression.

Yet, colorful or at least as varied as that development has proven to be, the word Hijab had already been developing in still other directions. These other directions aren't as visible as the one taken by Hijab as face veil, but they are no less significant.

These other directions come to light in the Qur'an itself. In at least two of the word's appearances there, it takes an ethical direction. Hijab denotes the consequence for those who willfully deafen themselves to the Qur'an's voice as proclaimed through prophet Muhammad. Here is one instance:

When you, Muhammad, recite the Qur'an, we put between you and those who scoff at the Hereafter an invisible veil [hijab]. (*sura al-isra'* 17:45)

It's possible to conclude from an example like this that Islam is all about getting on the right, favored side of the ethical Hijab. God himself is seen as upholding the ethical exclusion, the drawing of a difference in which believers in the life to come are on one side, disbelievers on the other. We can find parallels in our own Scriptures. Think of the gulf that divides the rich man from Lazarus, for instance.

Yet in *sura al-shura* 42:51, we discover a new meaning for Hijab, one we could call ontological (referring to our status as beings). For here we discover that all of us, believers and disbelievers, virgins and interlopers, prophet's wives and rowdy wedding guests, find ourselves lumped together on the "wrong" side. It's not that good and evil have been muddled by this lumping, however. It's that Hijab now denotes a necessary distinction between God and his creation, a creation that includes saints and sinners alike:

For it is not fitting for mere human beings that God should speak to them directly, face to face but instead either by inspiration [understood either as a suggestion or as a literal "audition," such as prophet Muhammad experienced] or from behind a Hijab or by the sending of a prophet inspired to convey, through God's permission, what God wills. For God is beyond all creation in his height, beyond all creation in his generosity.

One hadith explains the phrase "from behind a Hijab" as follows: "His veil is light. Were God to withdraw it, the splendor of his face would consume everything that comes within his sight." So while Hijab marks the infinite distance between God and ourselves ("infinite" as viewed from our side of the screen), Hijab also signifies the divine mercy. Trespassing cannot threaten God, but it would inevitably destroy the trespasser. We can think of parallels with our own Scriptures. God descends on Mt. Sinai in fire and smoke to hide his face from the Israelites lest they be consumed. Only Moses can penetrate the veil. We'll look at the Christian parallel later on in this chapter.

Set beside these examples, the first Hijab verse we looked at may now in retrospect look refreshingly concrete. Tactless wedding guests and a wall to keep them out of the bride's bedroom! If only this particular meaning of Hijab had stopped right there!

But history says otherwise. A meaning at first confined to Muhammad's own family situation spreads out to cover all Muslim women everywhere, at all times, including our own. Spreads out both to protect and to smother. For according to Muslim feminists, Hijab as face veil has always been ambiguous, as if from the start two opposed meanings were covered by the word. The face veil is seen from one standpoint as protecting Muhammad's wives and then all Muslim women from intrusion and disparagement, but then from another as repressing them. It is seen from one standpoint as defining women's identity as Muslims, then from another as erasing it. It is seen as excluding intrusive males not of the family, then (especially in Western eyes) as provoking, enticing them.

Ambiguity does not cloud the ethical meaning of Hijab, however. Those of us finding ourselves divided from sinners are reassured that we have indeed, with God's help, accomplished a true (not a hypocritical) self-yielding. And while those others of us finding ourselves divided from true Muslims may for a time gratify the perverse streak in us, we'll see things differently at the Last Judgment. For then our folly and self-destructiveness will be clearly revealed. As for the ontological Hijab that separates all of us from God, this is the clearest, least ambiguous barrier of all. Even to imagine ourselves on the other side of that barrier is to invite self-idolatry. Yet these meanings, rich as they are, do not exhaust the concept of Hijab.

What remains to be said about Hijab is not a meaning explicitly given the term in the Qur'an. Yet this remainder gathers up in its many folds a fundamental Qur'anic understanding. The Hijab in question is foundational, and refers to a necessary tension introduced into the fabric of creation by the Maker himself.

This tension is expressed by another Qur'anic word, *zawj*, which means "one of a pair." While God himself is an indivisible unity (Tauhid), everything in God's creation is paired. Dualism is a necessary characteristic of all created things. Says the Qur'an:

And of all things we have created pairs [plural *azwaj*]. Perhaps you will reflect on this fact. (*sura al-dhariyat* 51:49)

The zawj is usually interpreted in terms of sexual difference and complementarity. Human nature itself is seen as one (as the unifying constituent and marker of our created reality, body and soul), but human functioning and flourishing—and by analogy the functioning and flourishing of everything else in creation—is seen in terms of pairing, primarily but not exclusively as male and female.

Muslim feminists base many of their arguments for gender equality between men and women on the way the Qur'an talks about the zawj. Their argument is that insofar as men and women form azwaj, they are equally essential and equally dependent on each other.

But zawj can have another purpose. It can help us see the point of a further meaning of Hijab, as that which maintains the identity of each thing within an overarching common call to Islam. Islam means self-yielding, but it does not mean self-suppression or self-immolation. What is yielded is the false, heedless, obsessed, idolatrous self. What is gained in return is the true self, visible only when it has become truly transparent to God. Zawj enhances this additional meaning of Hijab by suggesting that our individual human differences, expressed as a complementarity of azwaj or pairs, are fundamental to creation itself. The pairs may be seen sexually as well as in terms of gender roles, but not necessarily so. There are many ways by which one human being can find himself or herself complemented or completed in another.

A second way to express the value of our differences, and the usefulness of the term Hijab as a marker of that value, is to look at the way the Qur'an addresses us. The Qur'an addresses the free will of every human creature. The address itself, while powerfully commanding, is never bullying. The Qur'an seeks to persuade, not to browbeat; to invite, not to overwhelm. The Qur'an's urgency comes from divine concern, not from divine eagerness to dominate. So we respond freely—perhaps wrongly, but always freely. Our disobedience is our own, as is our Islam. Our entry into the "right" side of the ethical Hijab (if we are so blessed as to get that far!) does not crush our will or erase our difference from others. Our entry perfects our will, by connecting it with its true complement, the will of God. Our entry perfects our personality, by connecting it with its true complement in the perfected personalities of others. It's as if a Hijab accompanies us into God's light, marking the true particularity of what is you or me. Without this Hijab, the completion of our creation as human beings is impossible.

At least one passage in the Qur'an directly expresses this sense of our necessary complementarity:

O humankind! We created you all to be different, as male and female. And we made you into different tribes and nations so that you could come to know each other. But the best of you all are those most attentive [ataqum: from taqwa, as adjective in the intensive form] to me. And I will know this, since God is all knowing, all wise. (sura al-hujurat 49:13)

This verse follows two others in which God castigates humankind for its usual ways of dealing with difference: meanness, sarcasm, slander, scapegoating. The term Hijab (if it were to appear in these previous two verses) would probably work ethically, dividing those given over to such evils from those who have resisted them. Then in the verse quoted directly above, God sets up a different kind of Hijab: one that stimulates not only mutual understanding but self-understanding as well, since it is through the other that we come to know ourselves. Our difference—our identity—depends upon the difference and identity of others.

It's this final Hijab, the foundational one, the one that marks our perfected, hence complementary individualities, that I see in my mind's eye when I think back on gatherings of Muslim women I've witnessed at the Islamic Center and elsewhere. As worn by the women at the Islamic Center, gathered for Friday prayer or bringing in their favorite dishes for a Ramadan fast-breaking or taking their turns as audiences or speakers at assemblies both intra-Muslim and inter-faith—this foundational Hijab becomes a sign of complementary human difference. A sign of what we pass into, neither to dominate nor to erase, neither to be absorbed into nor to be annihilated by. We pass into a difference in which relationships are perfected. The Hijabs swirling around at the kinds of gatherings mentioned above speak to us of the individual differences of the wearers. They close off easy access, false identity. At the same time the Hijabs make the differences available for fruitful relationship. The foundational Hijab discloses and veils at the same time— not in enticement, but in testimony to the principle of complementarity by which God brought all things into being.

Envisioning the foundational Hijab placed between the sexes and between tribes and nations—and between individuals and religions too—depends upon envisioning the ontological Hijab separating all of us from God. Placing ourselves sincerely and forthrightly before this ontological Hijab relativizes and purifies our foundational stance before every other individual in the rest of creation. For while we cannot pass over into God, God can pass over into us. The ontological Hijab is transparent from God's side. To know ourselves as we are known by him is our goal. God imparts that knowledge to the "best of us," to "the most attentive." Illuminated by that insight, our true differences and the Hijabs that mark them emerge in all their radiance, like Yasmin's beautiful garments at Friday prayers. All other Hijabs, especially those woven by egoism in all its self-destructive forms, burn and disintegrate in the light of God's face—revealing only emptiness behind.

◆ The Veil of the Temple ◆

The wearing of a head veil by women has a tradition in Christianity, but it is different from the tradition in Islam, and is certainly nothing as central to the continuing identity of Muslims both male and female as the Hijab is.

It's true that the Hijab as face veil recalls the centuries-long practice of Christian women religious, primarily Catholic but of other denominations as well, of wearing a head scarf or wimple, along with a long ankle-length outer gown that resembles the jilbab.

Still honored in many countries is women's ancient practice of covering their hair when entering church.

When we look into the biblical justification for this practice, we find parallelisms with Islam's struggles between a prophetic egalitarianism and accommodation to cultural practice, with women used in both instances as a symbolic field of battle.

For example, St. Paul declares in 1 Corinthians 11:5 that "any woman who prays or prophesies with her head unveiled disgraces her head." Part of his argument rests on his previous assertion in 1 Corinthians that the head covering is a sign of women's God-given inferiority to men. "I want you to understand that Christ is the head of every man, and the husband is the head of his wife; and God is the head of Christ" (1 Cor. 11:3). Is this the same St. Paul who declares, in Galatians 3:28: "There is no longer Jew or Greek, there is no longer slave or free, there is no longer male and female"?

But while establishing women's rights is an ongoing struggle within both religions, that struggle is not symbolized within both by the face veil itself. Within Islam yes, within Christianity, no.

This fact makes our return to Christianity with insights gained from studying the Hijab more challenging. If the Hijab as face veil cannot fully cover our passage, we'll have to look further to find what can.

The word Hijab itself can help us. As used in the Arabic version of the New Testament available to me, the word brings us very close to the ethical and ontological meanings of Hijab as we identified them in the Qur'an. Having done that, it dramatically points us in another direction.

In my Arabic version of all three synoptic Gospels, the word Hijab is used for only one purpose, to translate the Greek word *katapetasma*. *Katapetasma* refers to the inner curtain of the Temple that separated the holy place from the holy of holies. Only the High Priest could penetrate that inner curtain on the Day of Atonement. But according to the evangelists the Hijab receives a new significance through the passion of Jesus—as the sign of Jesus having opened up access to the holy of holies to all.

Mark's Gospel is representative. There, Jesus "gave a loud cry and breathed his last." And at that instant: "The curtain (Hijab) of the temple was torn in two, from top to bottom" (15:37-38). Then, as if responding to both events (though realistically he could have taken in only the first), the centurion says: "Truly this man was God's son!" Matthew and Luke in their own ways augment the effect of the tearing of the Hijab, Matthew making it central to a series of cataclysms that follow on Jesus' death, Luke placing the tearing dramatically before it.

In each evangelist the Hijab stands for a fundamental difference or separation whose breeching or tearing is inaugurated by Jesus' death.

This significance is clarified by three other instances where Hijab is used in my Arabic version of the New Testament, all of these found in the Letter to the Hebrews. Again, Hijab translates the Greek word katapetasma.

At 6:19-20, God guarantees his promise to Abraham through a

. . . hope that enters the inner shrine behind the curtain [Hijab], where Jesus, a forerunner on our behalf, has entered, having become a high priest forever according to the order of Melchizedek.

It isn't a question of a literal tearing of the Hijab, but of the passing through it by Jesus the high priest. The cultic practice has been maintained, with this key difference, that now we, in the form of that "hope," enter the shrine after the "forerunner." The Hijab is intact. What has changed is our own status in relation to it.

In Hebrews 9:3 the holy of holies "behind the Hijab" is described in detail, as if, having now passed through or behind the Hijab ourselves, we stand in the position of Jesus the high priest himself. Following the steps of this great forerunner we stand directly in the presence of God.

But the fullest development of Christian Hijab occurs in Hebrews 10:19–22:

Therefore, my friends, since we have confidence to enter the sanctuary by the blood of Jesus, by the new and living way he opened for us through the curtain [Hijab] (that is, through his flesh), . . . let us approach with a true heart in full assurance of faith. . . .

It isn't just a matter of revolutionizing the cult by providing access to the holy of holies to those previously excluded. The

Hijab is the flesh itself: no longer a mark of our separation from God but the very means of our new intimacy with him, through the death and resurrection of his Son.

In Christ, the Hijab of the flesh is not torn and discarded as if it had no value. It is resurrected. The Hijab disappears as barrier and impediment, returns as fulfilled identity in communion with God and the rest of God's creation.

Let's pause a moment and look at some consequences of this transformation of the Hijab as flesh, first for our understanding of Islam, then for our understanding of our own Christian identity, and finally for the relationship between the two religions.

Islam first. We spoke earlier about an ontological Hijab in Islam that draws an unbridgeable distinction between God on one side of being, and creation, including all humanity, on the other. Yet ontological Hijab covers only our own side of things. There can be no barrier impenetrable to God, among whose Beautiful Names is that of *al-basir* or the One who sees everything.

Returning to Christianity from the Hijab helps us appreciate our difference from Islam here, at that place in the temple where the ontological Hijab is hung. In Islam there is no passing through that ontological Hijab, not even by a high priest. In Christianity Jesus our brother leads the way forward, and we in hope follow behind to the very Holy of Holies itself.

What is being claimed here? That we have been absorbed into God, have become indistinguishable from him, or have become gods ourselves? None of those, of course, though it can be a very healthy challenge for us Christians to explain to our Muslim friends why not.

Our study of the Hijab has strengthened our own effort to explain why not. It has done so by opening up the possibility of foundational Hijab. Foundational Hijab asserts that individual difference stimulates self-understanding through complementarity. We grow in our understanding of ourselves as God's creations not in isolation from others but through passing over to those whose individualities complement our own.

Passing through or beyond the Hijab of the temple by following at the heels of Jesus the forerunner doesn't erase our difference from God or our fellow creatures. It confirms and glorifies our individual difference in our own redeemed flesh. The resurrection initiated by Jesus is a resurrection not of isolated spiritual heroes but of a community of sinners, now washed clean, each indubitably him or herself, but each complementing the other. The sacrament of marriage gives a hint of what such complementarity might mean. Two people become one not by being absorbed into each other, but by allowing the other to develop into that particular imaging of God that he or she has been given to be. What is true of two is true of all. Imaging God means uniting our own particular imaging with every other, so that in the end the picture of God may be complete.

A clue to the communal nature of the redemption longed for can be seen in the way the writer of Hebrews in 10:19,22 uses the word "friends" along with the first person plural. "We enter . . ." "Let us approach . . . etc." What binds these friends, what makes them one, is that each approaches the sanctuary with a "true heart in full assurance of faith." They don't all melt together into an undifferentiated mass as they pass through this Hijab of the flesh. Nor do they dissolve indistinguishably into the ocean of the godhead. They become more recognizable in their individuality, more of what each one was meant to be. Each wears, as he or she emerges into the light of God, the new Hijab, the redeemed flesh of his or her divinized difference.

As with so much else about our faith that demands imagination, Dante has said it best. I quote Dante here partly to balance my previous reference to him in Chapter One, where his depiction of Muhammad in hell is perhaps the low point of the *Divine Comedy*.

Having at last reached paradise, Dante is amazed to discover that the redeemed souls, while residing together in one community in the highest heaven or Empyrean, nevertheless speak to him from the particular place or sphere in the lower heavens to which their individual merit assigns them. The differences among the redeemed, far from being causes of suspicion or envy, are sources of delight, since each soul understands the indispensable glory of its place within the whole which is the body of Christ. At first, Dante can't fathom this non-rivalrous joy. Meeting Piccarda Donati, a soul residing on the lowest sphere of heaven, that of the moon, Dante asks her whether she doesn't seek a place higher up. Piccarda, along with the other souls on that sphere who hear Dante's question, smiles at the naive absurdity of the question. Then, as Dante says, she

> . . . answered me with such joy
> that she seemed to burn in the first fire of love:
> "Brother, the strength of the love of God
> quiets our heart, and makes us desire
> only what we have, not thirst for something else."
> Paradiso, III, 69–72 (author's translation)

Emboldened by Dante, maybe we can glimpse between Christianity and Islam too the possibility of a delighting in necessary difference. Each religion delighting in its particular call by

God while at the same time sharing in the complementary richness provided by the other. Each religion would recognize that the fullness—the salaam—imagined, promised, longed for, and achieved in Islam is necessarily different from the redemption imagined, promised, longed for, and achieved in Christianity. They would see that there is a Hijab between one religion's goal and the other's (that is, between salvation and salaam). But where previously they saw the Hijab as a barrier, even as a wall erected between their opposing armies, now they see it as the invitation to a completeness not possible within either religion alone. A completeness which does not rob either religion of its distinctiveness, but which makes the distinctiveness all the more brilliantly necessary.

The grandeur of such a vision would probably escape Donald Duck and his three nephews, but not the vision's joyful, even playful adventurousness. In Dante's *Paradiso* also, the saints cannot contain their smiles.

TWELVE · *Takbir and*
"Hallowed be thy Name"

◆ The Holy Spirit Threads Three Beads ◆

"*Allahu akbar!* (God, there is none greater!)"

As the mourners in Rochester's Islamic Center chanted these words, I joined in.

I hadn't planned to attend a funeral that day. I had come to the Islamic Center for a meeting of the Muslim-Catholic Alliance, the committee formed to implement the historic accord signed in May 2003 between the Roman Catholic Diocese of Rochester and Rochester's Islamic community.

While I was standing in the Islamic Center's vestibule waiting for the members of the committee to gather, I'd heard a Muslim friend say, to me and to Louis, a fellow Catholic and committee member standing beside me, "Can you fellows help? We need a couple more people."

Help with what? I wondered.

Then someone else said something about a body in a casket that needed to be brought into the Center. Louis and I went outside. Sure enough, a hearse had pulled into the Center's parking lot. A couple of men had gathered behind it, easing a plain wooden casket from the interior. Louis and I grasped one of the casket's side handles and helped bear it up the Center's steps into the masjid or prayer area. We placed the casket gently on the rug just to the right of the mihrab or prayer niche, facing Mecca. Then Louis and I stepped back while a group of Muslim men formed a line in front of us. At this point we all began to chant *"allahu akbar!"* in response to the imam or prayer leader, who repeatedly cried out *"Takbir!"* ("Let us extol him!").

Later, during the meeting of the Muslim-Catholic Alliance, my mind kept wandering from the proceedings to my experience just before, at the funeral. I was struck by the extraordinary generosity and trust of the Muslims who had invited Louis and me, two Catholic Christians, to participate so intimately in the burial of one of their brothers.

I was also struck by the appropriateness of the chant *"allahu akbar"* in the face of death and loss. That one little phrase said more than lengthy sermons about the faithfulness and everlastingness of God as a refuge in the midst of our ever-changing lives.

¡O Dios, tu eres grande! (O God, you are great!)
These were the words in the refrain of a song I found myself singing just a few hours later on the very same day at a prayer service in Spanish I'd been invited to at an inner-city parish.

The evening was warm, so we set up chairs in a circle on a bit of grass outside the church. We sang, prayed spontaneously in a simultaneous weaving of ecstatic voices, read Scripture, commented on it, sang some more, prayed some more, and at the end gave testimonies of God's goodness to us and others.

I was silent at first during the spontaneous prayer, uncertain about what my heart wanted to say and self-conscious about my capacity to say it in Spanish. But the shuttling of voices in and out around me drew me into the fabric. I found myself praying for all my Muslim friends, and especially for those who had buried their loved one earlier that day. I also prayed in gratitude and wonder for my Hispanic friends. They'd been as generous as the Muslims in inviting me, an Anglo outsider, to share in the intimacy of their worship. Both of these generosities within a single day!

But the words of the song were what really captured my imagination, *O Dios, tu eres grande*. As I sang them, I was amazed that they carried a meaning so similar to the *"allahu akbar"* I'd just chanted at the Islamic Center. True, we weren't gathered at the church to celebrate a funeral, but we were praising God's fidelity and care in the midst of change and difficulty, just as the Muslims were. We were doing so during a blessed moment where differences in religion and ethnicity didn't matter.

For my testimony afterward, I told my Hispanic friends about hearing and chanting the same words of praise just a couple of hours before at the Islamic Center.

"That just shows," one of my Hispanic friends said, "that we are truly one in the care of the one God."

"May I ask what you're writing?"

A week or so had passed. I was sitting on the aisle seat of a small commuter airplane headed for Washington, where I was going to attend a conference. On my lap was a pad of paper. At the top of the first page I'd scrawled in large block letters the title "God is Great in Rochester." I hadn't written much else. I knew I wanted to describe my experience at the Islamic Center and at the church for possible publication in our local newspaper. But I wasn't quite sure how to begin. The one thing

I did feel sure of was that the experience itself was over and done with, ready to be put in words that would give it (I hoped) a smooth finish.

But God was writing the story, not I. And God had not done working with the material. God still saw potential in it.

It was in the midst of my puzzlement about how to start that I heard the voice quoted above. I glanced up and caught the eye of a woman sitting across the aisle. She quickly explained that she had noticed I was trying to write something and that when she saw the title she couldn't stop wondering what it was all about. Would I mind telling her?

Maybe if I hadn't felt a little stuck I would have minded. As it was, I was glad to have a distraction. And I was also gratified and encouraged by the woman's interest.

Yet her interest began to seem exaggerated. She couldn't stop thanking me. And then she began to weep. Something was happening here that couldn't be explained by satisfied curiosity merely.

I was right. In a conversation that lasted the duration of the flight, the woman explained that she and her husband and child were on their way to Florida to go to her mother's funeral. Her mother, like the woman's sister a year or so before, had died of cancer. The woman had not been able to forgive God for these deaths, had not been able to go to church, had not been able to pray. But somehow the title and then the story I told her about *Allahu akbar* and *O Dios, tu eres grande* had broken down a wall of resistance. She now felt that it was God who needed to forgive her, not the other way around.

Just before the plane landed, she, a Protestant, and I, a Catholic, said a prayer together, not just for a continuation of the peace about her mother's death that our chance encounter had brought her, but for a transformation in her relationship with God.

Afterward, as I rode the airport bus into downtown Washington, I couldn't get my mind on the upcoming conference. One thing I kept thinking about instead was God's lavishness. Just when I'd thought that the experience beginning in the Islamic Center had taken a shape that was surprising enough, God had added another dimension to it. God piled coincidence on top of coincidence—if coincidence was the right word. The connection between the Muslims at the Center, the Hispanics at the church prayer meeting, and the Protestant woman on the airplane was certainly unexpected, but to say it was merely coincidental would be hard to prove.

There was another explanation, equally hard to prove, perhaps, but truer to the actual feel of events. More persuasive to me was the belief that connecting the three events was a kind of pulse or dynamism normally hidden from my view. Or not so much normally hidden from my view as normally unnoticed by me, because of my tendency to be distracted by unimportant things. It seemed to me that I had been privileged to witness—and to act briefly as a conduit for—a powerful working of God that had moved from the Muslim mourners at the Islamic Center on that certain day when I and my Catholic friend Louis "happened" to be present, had passed over into the Hispanic parishioners of the downtown church, then had leaped overland to Georgia via my Protestant aisle mate.

Yet this force, for all its seeming arbitrariness or playfulness, had a single purpose: to bring consolation, confidence, healing, unity. It didn't simply deposit its balm in individual empty containers, however. It seemed to use each place of healing as a point of further transmission. The healing force did not originate with me. It was already in motion when the mourners had asked Louis and me to help bear the body into the mosque. It did not stop with me either. Perhaps the Protestant woman was the next chosen conduit. Perhaps some of the Hispanics who'd been at the prayer service or some of the Muslims at the funeral had already been bearing it along. Who could name all the people already and still to be passed over to and from as the divine impulse sped along, fanning out without limit through diverse hearts? Who could say?

Only the God who could not, cannot be contained.

◆ The Many Meanings of Takbir ◆

Allahu akbar.

The usual translation, "God is great" (or sometimes one sees: "God, there is none greater" or even "God is the greatest") doesn't do the statement justice, doesn't bring out its full flavor.

Literally *Allahu akbar* means: "God, he [is] beyond greatness" or more accurately (if also awkwardly): "God, he cannot be compared in greatness with anything else."

The point is that akbar represents the intensive form of the Arabic adjective, a form that doesn't exist in English. In English we can compare things, saying that one thing is greater than another or that one thing is the greatest among all other things like it. But we can't say that a thing, in terms of one of its qualities, exists outside all comparison whatsoever, making it impossible even to say that the thing is the best of the lot. Allahu akbar means that, when it comes to greatness—from the root *kabara*, meaning "to be bigger than another," hence weightier, more authoritative—God is not in the same league with anything else, not even with the things we normally think of as "great": great mountains, great oceans, great people.

Allahu akbar is a way of separating God from all ordinary measurements. Woe to anyone who would blur the distinction in his or her own favor. One of the worst things that can be said about another person in the Qur'an is that he (or she) *istakbara or* "considers himself great," a reflexive form of kabara that connotes rank arrogance, the stealing of God's prerogative. We can risk comparing ourselves with each other, because we are all made of the same stuff. But God lies outside the reach of our language, relativizing such greatness as we think distinguishes created things and revealing the actual smallness of that greatness, so dependent is it on what is eternally outside it, on what cannot be compared to it.

Allahu akbar derives from the humility enjoined by this recognition. But the mood of the statement is less penitential than celebratory. Allahu akbar is a public proclamation of a glad iconoclasm, a joyful recognition that despite all that we in our arrogance may say and think, God truly is God, truly beyond our petty and self-serving manipulations, beyond our anger at him, beyond our doubt of him, beyond our refusals to believe in him. No image, no language, not even praise, can contain him. He is big in a way that makes all our notions of bigness small. Even to say he is beyond us in greatness cannot contain him.

Caution! We can get big-headed just by the ease with which we can name our limitations. Granted that our created separateness puts a gulf between us and God measured from our side of things. Seen from God's side, however—absurd as it is to imagine God's having a "side"—there can be no corresponding distance, no "gulf." All that we can know about God comes through God's unceasing ayat or signs, especially those ayat which are the very lines of the Qur'an. Relevant among them is that ayah or line that says: "I am closer to you than your jugular vein" (*sura gaf* 50:16). This ayah tells us that God's distance from us is no less absolute than his intimacy. In the same breath that we proclaim the gulf between him and us, we're obliged to proclaim his unimaginable closeness.

Allahu akbar is spoken in wonder and gratitude for the distance and the closeness at the same time. God's presence encompasses—and exceeds—both. And not just on the big occasions of our lives, but at each second of every day. That is why for most Muslims Allahu akbar is a key phrase in their private dhikr or remembering. Allahu akbar marks every communal occasion too. Allahu akbar is a prescribed phrase at Salat or the five daily public prayers, at weddings, at funerals (as we have seen), at the Shahadah or confession of faith of a new Muslim, during the Hajj or pilgrimage to Mecca. It is used informally on all occasions where something has happened or someone has said or done something that does honor to God or that invites praise. For example, I heard it used frequently at a recent regional meeting of the Islamic Society of North America instead of applause, to show community approval of particularly insightful speeches.

On these public occasions, the imam or person leading the prayer or in some other way in charge of proceedings evokes the community's response by calling out, "Takbir." Takbir is based on another form of kabarah that means "call something great" or "extol." As Takbir, though, it becomes a verbal noun with a performative feel. Takbir doesn't simply mean "extolling." It means "Let him be extolled," that is, "let him be called great." To which the response is "Allahu akbar." Takbir gathers up our desire to express publicly an intuition of divine presence that cannot be expressed because its referent, God, exceeds our capacity for expression. But what escapes our mind's capacity does not escape our hearts. Allahu akbar celebrates a reality, or rather reality itself, beyond and above the turmoil of our lives, while at the same time intimately present within it. The heart bears up under the apparent contradiction better than the mind can. And even expands in the process, opening to sense new horizons where God's passings-over flash like lightning from one opened heart to another.

But hearts don't open in a spirit of spectatorship, as at a supremely successful divine feat or performance. God's greatness is not praised for what the praise itself says (or tries to say) about God, but for what the praise says about God's care for us, even in ordinary moments when someone or something—even a scribbled title on a pad resting on a fellow-passenger's lap—can suddenly open a passage for God's healing presence.

I have a fantasy in which a Muslim with a big enough heart "happens" to be sitting next to me near the window on that flight to Washington. He overhears the conversation between the Protestant woman and me. His only contribution is one word: "Takbir."

◆ Hallowed Be Thy Name ◆

Returning to Christianity from Takbir brings me home to the Lord's Prayer and enlivens my understanding of the phrase "hallowed be thy name" as a Christian equivalent.

Goodness knows the phrase needs enlivening.

Even after all these years I keep hearing the antique word "hallowed" as if it were "hollowed." (In the same way as I still sing nostalgically of that fabulous land floating on faraway seas, "My country Tizzivthy.")

Of course "hallowed" comes from "holy," not "hollow." "Holy" in the sense in which Jesus was using it when he gave us the Lord's Prayer refers to a stripping away of what is unholy, of what is not-God, from what should be God's own, in this case God's name. The form is petitionary, echoing the cry of the Hebrew prophets for the vindication of God's name through the restoration of Israel. Put in the form of a prayer for the use of Christ's own disciples, "hallowed be thy name" (or in more modern fashion "may your name be holy") is a direct cry for access to that holy name, here and now—and therefore for a shedding of all the egotism and injustice that have encumbered it through our complicity with evil.

For the French mystic Simone Weil, the petition "hallowed be thy name" expresses a longing for what is real, not for what we take to be real:

> This name is holiness itself; there is no holiness outside it; it does not therefore have to be hallowed. In asking for its hallowing we are asking for something that exists eternally, with full and complete reality, so that we can neither increase nor diminish it, even by an infinitesimal fraction. To ask for that which exists, that which exists really, infallibly, eternally, quite independently of our prayer, that is the perfect petition.[x]

According to Weil, "hallowed be thy name" is structured by a paradoxical twist. We pray for what our prayer cannot name. Allahu akbar is structured in a similar way, though it is more acclamation than petition. Both prayers express a desire for escape from the self and its fantasies, so that an opening to God's healing activity can be made.

In logical form, though, Allahu akbar most resembles the famous "ontological proof" of St. Anselm (1033–1109) for the existence of God: "God is that than which no greater can be thought." This proof has, over the centuries, exercised and often frustrated theologians and philosophers alike. But its difficulties are greatly eased if we look at it through the lens provided by Allahu akbar. William H. Shannon, in his *Anselm: The Joy of Faith*, reminds us that Anselm uses the "proof" not as a weapon in a logical argument, but as way of expressing and therefore satisfying our longing for God. Allahu akbar. God is beyond our categories of greatness, beyond all categories of thought, yet given to us through faith. By means of the "proof" Anselm prays, as Simone Weil believes Jesus did in the "hallowed be thy name" of the Lord's Prayer, for what really exists, independently of all our notions of existence. To pray in this way, whether through the "proof" or through the paradox of "hallowed be thy name," is not to erect a triumph to human logic but to use logic as a ladder that we gladly push away, in confidence that we are not left spinning in a void but are sustained by divine mercy. The Qur'an has its own graphic way of describing the desired outcome of our leap of faith: "And hold fast all together by the rope which God stretches out to you, and be not divided among you . . ." (*sura al-'imran* 3:103).

This Qur'anic quotation, and the sequence Takbir—Allahu akbar, reminds us that the appeal to a God-beyond-greatness is not a solitary's utterance but a communal action, a communal prayer. It is liturgy. When we say "hallowed be thy name," we say it in community, whether we're alone or in a group. It isn't "my" Father in heaven, it's "our" father. For Anselm too the "proof" was offered as the focus of prayer not just for himself but for the monks of his community at Bec. Similarly for Muslims. Takbir is the imam's or leader's call to the ummah of believers. Allahu akbar is chanted back gratefully and enthusiastically by all. The prayer, in whatever form we say it, is a prayer that encourages unity.

A unity that, because of what Christians and Muslims both believe about the God who enjoins it upon his creation, cannot be restricted to certain members of that creation. At every moment God is passing over to all that he has made to heal and sustain it, and bids us acknowledge his activity, not for his praise only but also for our encouragement, so that we will want to pass over too, and so in our turn heal and sustain the creation entrusted to us as God's kalifa or vice-regents (*sura al-bakarah* 2:30).

Yet such a mission seems to mock us. In the Qur'anic verse just referred to, God no sooner announces his intention to create humankind as his kalifa than the angels speak up:

"Will you put on earth a creature who will surely do all kinds of wrong and spill blood, while we are the ones who praise and glorify you?"

God's answer: "I know what you do not."

There's been much Muslim discussion of this exchange. The majority view seems to be that the angels aren't speaking out of resentment but out of bewilderment. Lacking free will themselves, they can't conceive of a divine plan which has as its centerpiece the granting of free will, let alone the granting of it to a creature of mere clay such as ourselves.

I think we can sympathize with the angels. God's intentions for us must remain a mystery. Because what we notice about ourselves is that we behave just as the angels said we would. We repeat the Lord's Prayer and cry Allahu akbar endlessly, yet manifestly God's will is not done, manifestly his supremacy is flouted, manifestly his healing power is blocked. We cannot satisfy our desire to spill each other's blood. As for the differences among us Christians and Muslims, they don't invite us to search out our complementarities but instead instigate us to demonize each other or at best to keep each other at a suspicious distance.

And yet: "I know what you do not." Just when we least expect it, at a Muslim funeral, for example, the divine energy surges through us, picking us up, carrying us along willy-nilly until we discharge that energy into diverse Christian hearts, according to a schedule and plan totally unknown to us. The differences between Muslims and Christians, or between Anglos and Latinos, or between Catholics and Protestants, don't come crashing down, however. The foundational Hijab referred to in the previous chapter is never discarded, but becomes instead a kind of conductor of energy or else a screen transparent to the light suddenly beaming through it from a source we can never look at directly—and probably couldn't look at directly without being destroyed. By means of that energy or that light, patterns of congruence are revealed in us. The patterns suggest a shared gratitude to a God in whom all things are possible, even the unity of creatures such as ourselves, creatures formed of clay, prone to violence, true, but nevertheless breathed upon by the divine ruh or spirit and so not only lifted up ourselves but also lifting up in our turn all creation, including even the puzzled angels, in praise.

Takbir!

Conclusion

"Well, yes," you may be saying after the enthusiastic finale of that last chapter on Takbir. "Treasuring our differences with Muslims is certainly better than fearing them. The very nature of God as Trinity, so far as we can understand that nature, invites us to venture past our barriers and boundaries into wider and deeper relationships with all God's people. Without differences the whole idea of relationship would be meaningless. Unity clearly should have nothing to do with uniformity. And yet . . . and yet . . ."

Let me finish your thought: And yet we live in a world that expends a tremendous amount of energy turning differences into divisions and thus breaking relationships. Injustice follows, and all manner of violence. Through the fog of fear thus created, Muslims come to look more and more like a cursed people, prone to extremism, totalitarianism, suicidal fanaticism. How can we possibly pierce through that fog produced on such a grand scale by governments and fanned abroad by a sensation-loving media?

Alas, *Meeting Islam: A Guide for Christians* offers you no easy way of dispersing that fog, no quick blueprint for wholesale change in human behavior. But *Meeting Islam: A Guide for Christians* does urge you to take the step increasing numbers of people in Rochester are taking. They screw their courage to the sticking point and venture forth even on snowy Upstate winter nights to attend talks and discussions on Islam sponsored by the ecumenical Commission on Christian-Muslim Relations and by the Muslim-Catholic Alliance and held at the Islamic Center. I love to stand at the front door of the Center along with Muslims and other Christians to welcome newcomers to such events. I see my own face of fourteen years ago reflected in the anxious faces of those approaching the Center for the first time. I see those faces relax as mine must have in response to the warm greetings the newcomers receive as they enter. Then later, upstairs, during the discussion period after the evening's presentation ("Faith and Worship in Islam," "Muhammad and the Qur'an," "Jihad in Islam and Christianity" are typical ones), I love to see those newcomers, now old-timers, put their concerns freely into words. I especially love to see them enjoying themselves and laughing. After a recent presentation, for example, somebody in the audience wanted to know whether it was true that in heaven Muslim men got to enjoy seventy-two virgins. The answer came back from the presenters that such passages had been twisted out of context and didn't at all suggest that God condoned orgies. A woman in the audience commented wryly, "I can see that. Having to cope with even one virgin doesn't sound like any picnic to me." The whole gathering, Muslims included, broke out in laughter. Every Christian in the room was truly "meeting Islam."

Can't you enjoy such experiences in your own community? Do inter-faith organizations like Rochester's ecumenical Commission on Christian-Muslim Relations and the Muslim-Catholic Alliance already exist where you live? Have you looked into the programs they offer? If there are no such organizations, what's to prevent you from getting together with fellow Christians and Muslims to found them? Meeting Islam needn't be and really oughtn't to be the solo experience it was for me back in 1992. As an adventure in relationships, meeting Islam really ought to take shape in communal settings, in conformity with both religions' emphasis on the sharing of God's gifts to all.

Whether your meeting Islam occurs through your own individual initiative or is supported by an inter-faith community's commitment, you'll still need encouragement along the way. For reasons mentioned directly above, and throughout this book, meeting Islam has its risks.

I have three words of advice about these risks. In their most stripped down form they are:

• Don't be afraid; • Be patient; • Have fun.

I'll end by developing each of these in more detail.

◆ "Peace be with you." ◆

"Don't be afraid" isn't a simple call for courage. It is a call for faith, the resurrected Jesus' own call. With it, he greets the disciples huddling behind locked doors for fear of reprisals from fellow Jews who put their master to death.

Question: Aren't the disciples a lot like many of us Christians in the United States at the present time, more concerned with our security than our salvation? Billions of dollars swell an already bloated defense budget presumably designed to keep us sealed off from the rest of the world and its "evil." The assumption is that this "evil" is a force completely outside us. All we have to do is put up a big enough wall and we'll be safe from it. But will we also be saved? Jesus effortlessly passed through the walls of the disciples' self-imposed prison in order to call them back into relationship. Having opened themselves to his grace and to the peace that flows from grace, the disciples found it no hard matter to open their prison house and fearlessly go forth to proclaim the Good News.

Can't we do the same, when it comes to Muslims? We can proclaim the Good News to them in our love of neighbor. We can cast out fear in confidence that Jesus walks with us into the mosque, as he walks with us everyplace else.

◆ "Beautiful Patience!" ◆

According to our Bible's version of the story of Joseph, the brothers sell Joseph to passing Midianites, then return to their father, Jacob, after staining Joseph's robe with blood. They pretend to know nothing of Joseph's fate. They claim they're not even sure the robe is his. When Jacob sees the robe, he leaps to the conclusion that Joseph has been killed by wild animals and in his great grief tears his garments, refusing to be consoled. (cf. Gen. 37:25–35)

The Qur'an's version of the Joseph story is different. The brothers return to Jacob with the bloody robe. But they tell their father that a wolf devoured him. Resentfully they add: "You won't believe us even though we're telling the truth."

Jacob no sooner glimpses the bloody robe than he sees through the brothers' plot:

"No, what really happened was nothing like that. Your minds have led you to connive this story. Beautiful patience! God is the one whose help I need against what you have described." (*sura Yusuf* 12:18)

"Beautiful patience"—the meaning is that God gives ayat or signs of his majesty and mercy in all things and events, including in apparent defeat or difficulty or contradiction. If we jump to our own conclusions, we'll misinterpret those signs, thus bringing grief upon ourselves (as Jacob did in the Bible story) and on others as well. But because the Qur'anic Jacob and Joseph too practice "beautiful patience," they are able eventually to heal the brothers' violence and treachery and to bring about salaam or fullness of life for the whole family.

"Beautiful patience" can be used in many situations in our meeting Islam, but one way in particular is important to emphasize. This has to do with Christians' and Muslims' differences of belief, particularly about Jesus' role in salvation—or indeed about the nature of salvation itself. Let's show "beautiful patience" when we come up against those differences!—neither tiptoeing around them nor anxiously trying to smooth them away. Certainly not arguing about them. Theologians on both sides find themselves deadlocked on these issues, most of them taking refuge in positions that declare the superiority of one faith over the other. "Beautiful patience" means that for the sake of meeting Islam and the human exchange that underlies all meetings, these differences, in their polemical expressions, can and should be tabled. Not that the differences aren't central to our capacity for relationship—as we said before, there can be no relationships without difference. We simply don't know each other well enough yet to talk about our differences in a tone that will bring joy to the Holy Spirit. That day will come, and efforts by Christians and Muslims to meet each other will hasten it. Meantime, "beautiful patience."

❖ "Rejoice in the Lord." ❖

Paul's words to the Philippians are as valid now as they ever were. There should be no long-faced Christians! We have an event no less significant than the Resurrection to celebrate, and the Resurrection is a fact of our lives each moment.

What I would add is that this resurrection joy is especially irrepressible whenever barriers come down. We have no record of what the disciples were feeling as they opened the door of the room where they'd been hiding and sallied forth into the sunshine, but in my own mind's eye I see them laughing. Why not? They'd just escaped prison!

So with us. Meeting Islam has its risks. It also has its indelible joys.

I end with one of my joys. I invite you to add your own!

I had spent the morning at the Islamic Center where the members of the Commission for Muslim-Christian Relations were putting finishing touches on a series of talks on Islam to be offered to the public beginning later that week.

Then in the early afternoon Dr. Shafiq and Aly Nahas, along with an imam from Turkey, carpooled in my car over to a city Catholic parish for a meeting of the Muslim-Catholic Alliance. Again the agenda was the planning of public presentations, only this time focused a little more narrowly on Catholic connections between the two faiths.

It was a good day, full of camaraderie and appreciation of each other's gifts and commitments to the cause of advancing inter-faith understanding.

The same group went back with me to the Islamic Center afterwards. The conversation was lively. I don't recall what brought my Muslim friends to this topic—probably something mentioned in passing at the afternoon's meeting—but the three of them no sooner got buckled in their seats than they wanted to know exactly what Christians meant by "original sin." (The concept is foreign to Islam. The Qur'anic argument goes: Humankind is erring, for sure. But God in his goodness has provided human beings with all they need in order to overcome their evil impulses. A God who provided them with less would not be a good God, would not even be God!) My friends weren't trying to challenge either me or the doctrine. They sincerely didn't understand the concept of "original sin" and so sought enlightenment.

Whether they were wise to seek that enlightenment from me was a question that crossed my mind. But now that they had sought it, I felt obliged to give whatever of it was in me. Besides, I relished this kind of discussion: irenic, without "agenda," where people of good will sincerely and eagerly strive to understand differences. In the terms of one of the metaphors used in this book, my Muslim friends were engaged in a passing over to Christianity. I wanted them to pass over just as far as they could go!

But it is not a good idea to try to dispense enlightenment while one is driving a car. At least it is not a good idea for me to do so. I became so absorbed in what I was saying as we drove along that I took two wrong turns. My companions finally had to tell me to shut up about original sin and concentrate on what I was doing until we reached the Islamic Center.

I could easily draw a cartoon of it: three intelligent Muslims trying their best to make heads or tails of a doctrine which we Christians treat with the utmost seriousness, but which, to my Muslim friends, according to whose holy Book the transgression in the Garden was almost immediately forgiven by God, looks like the silliest thing in the world; and their Christian driver, feverishly assembling the heavy chain of doctrine on the topic and meanwhile taking nearly every wrong turn possible between point A and point Z.

I felt embarrassed, amused, and delighted by that car ride. The Qur'an says that our life here on earth is not a joke, it is not to be taken lightly. But there is still room for laughter. We can laugh at our clumsy efforts to enjoy the diversity of God's creation in the way he intends us to.

I felt the fun, yes, but I also felt gratitude that in spontaneous moments such as this one I truly had been able to reach the goal I'd longed for, that of meeting Islam as a Christian.

Glossary

'Abd (Arabic: slave, servant) The Muslim who, worshiping in his or her outer, active, extroverted dimension, fulfills the requirements of the Five Pillars.

Adhan (Arabic: a call) The call to prayer, made five times a day from the mosque.

Alastu (Arabic: "Am I not. . .?") The first word of the Qur'anic ayah or line 7:172-3 from *sura al-a'raf* in which God asks the assembled seed of Adam, "Am I not your God?"

al-Ghazzali (d. 1111) Baghdad theologian who brought Sufism into harmony with the legal traditions of Islam.

Ali Cousin, ward, son-in-law of Muhammad. He became the Fourth Caliph in 656, but was murdered in 661. Shi'is revere him as the first imam (supreme spiritual leader) of the ummah or community.

Allah (Arabic: God) The name for "God" in the Arabic language and so used in the Arabic New Testament as well as in the Qur'an.

Allahu akbar (Arabic: "God, there is none greater") An exclamation of praise, gratitude, and humble acceptance of God's will.

Assalaam aleikum (Arabic: "peace be with you") Customary words of greeting by one Muslim to another. The reply is *waleikum assalaam* ("and peace be with you as well").

Ayah, plural *Ayat* (Arabic: "sign") A line or verse of the Qur'an. Each line is considered a "sign" of God's mercy. The sun, moon, stars, and all other natural phenomena are other such "signs."

Bismillah (Arabic: "In the name of Allah" or more fully: "In the name of Allah, the beneficent and merciful") The bismillah is a verbal formula found at the beginning of nearly every sura or chapter of the Qur'an. It precedes all Muslim prayers and is comparable in usage to "In the name of the Father, and the Son, and the Holy Spirit."

Dhikr (Arabic: "reminder, remembrance") One of the titles of the Qur'an. Also the technique of remembering God's name in Muslim devotion and Sufi practice.

Din (Arabic: "custom") Way of worship. Also "judgment" as in "Day of Judgment." Later used in the sense of "religion" in general.

Eid (Arabic: "feast, celebration") The two major feasts or festivals in Islam are *eid-al fitr* observed at the end of Ramadan and *eid-al-adha* at the end of the Hajj.

Fatihah (Arabic: "opening") The title of the first sura or chapter of the Qur'an. It is in the form of a model prayer to God and is recited frequently during Salat. Comparable to the "Our Father."

Five Pillars The five basic duties incumbent upon every Muslim: Shahadah, Salat, Zakat, Hajj, and Sawm.

Hadith (Arabic: "story") Reports of the words and deeds of prophet Muhammad.

Hafiz (Arabic: "one who memorizes") A *qari* or reciter who knows the Qur'an by heart.

Hajj (Arabic: "pilgrimage") The pilgrimage to Mecca which every Muslim must if possible perform at least once in his or her lifetime. One of the Five Pillars.

Hijab (Arabic: "door, barrier") The head scarf worn by Muslim women.

Hijrah (Arabic: "separation") The emigration of Muhammad and his followers to Medina in 622 CE.

Imam (Arabic: "pattern, leader") In Sunni Islam, the imam is the leader of prayer during Salat. In Shi'ah Islam, the imam is the descendant of Muhammad who becomes spiritual leader of the *ummah*.

Iman (Arabic: "faith") Whereas Islam refers primarily to practice, *Iman* refers to intellectual content: belief in Tauhid, in the angels and messengers, and in life after death.

'Isa The special name given Jesus in the Qur'an. The actual Arabic version of the name Jesus is "Yasu'."

Islam (Arabic: "handing oneself over") Primarily, the act of handing oneself over to God according to the ways summarized under the Five Pillars; secondarily, the name of the religion of Muslims.

Jihad (Arabic: "striving for a righteous goal") According to a hadith, Jihad is to be divided into Greater Jihad (the inward striving to purify one's motives) and the Lesser Jihad (the outer striving to defend the ummah from attack).

Ka'bah (Arabic: "cube") The square stone structure in Mecca marking the place of creation and of the Garden of Eden. Here Adam erected the first altar dedicated to God's worship. The site was rebuilt by Abraham and Ishmael, later polluted by the worship of idols, finally cleansed and restored to its primary use by Muhammad.

Kalam (Arabic: "speech, word") The active power of God as revealed in 'Isa's conception in the womb of the Virgin Mary. Kalam is used in an almost sacramental sense when it refers to the Qur'an. In later times, kalam referred to Muslim theology.

Khadijah Muhammad's first wife. She played a major role in the development of Islam by persuading the prophet that the revelations he was receiving were truly from God.

Khalifah (Arabic: "steward, vice-regent") The role assigned to humankind by God at creation, to be his "vice-regents" over the earth. Secondarily, the caliph or leader of the ummah, a title first assumed by Muhammad's friend and initial successor, Abu Bakr. The title was last used by the Ottoman rulers in Turkey.

La ilaha illa Allah (Arabic: "There is no god but God.") The first half of the Shahadah: "I confess that there is no God but God. . . ." The Muslim affirmation of monotheism.

Masjid (Arabic: "place for prostration") The designated space for public prayer. ("Mosque" is the antiquated English spelling of masjid.)

Mecca Site of the Ka'bah and of the yearly Hajj. Muhammad's birthplace.

Medina (Arabic: "city [of the prophet]") Formerly Yathrib, the town to which Muhammad and his followers emigrated in 622 CE to escape persecution in Mecca. Muhammad's place of burial.

Mi'raj (Arabic: "ladder, ascent") Muhammad's ascent through the seven heavens to the real Ka'bah, the *baitullah* or House of Allah.

Muslim (Arabic: "one who yields himself") Primarily, the one who yields him or herself to God according to the ways summarized by the Five Pillars. Secondarily, an adherent of the religion of Islam.

Qari (Arabic: "one who recites") A professional Qur'an reciter.

Qiblah (Arabic: "anything opposite") The direction of prayer towards Mecca.

Qur'an (Arabic: "reciting") Primary name for the Holy Book of the Muslims.

Rabi'a of Basra (d. 801 CE) - Female Sufi saint.

Ramadan Ninth month of the Muslim calendar. The first revelations came down to Muhammad while he was meditating in a cave near Mecca during this month. Muslims dedicate the month to fasting, to study of the Qur'an, and to prayers for forgiveness.

Ruh (Arabic: "breath, spirit") The creative power of God, especially active in endowing human beings with free will. Not seen as a "person" in the Trinitarian sense.

Rumi (1207–75) The founder of the Whirling Dervish Sufi order and Islam's greatest poet. His subject is the mystical love of God.

Sabr (Arabic: "patience"). A high Islamic virtue, reflecting the Qur'an's emphasis on moderation.

Salaam (Arabic: "peace, fullness of relationships") The state of safety or peace itself, as well as the greeting of peace; the perfection and perpetuation of the just ummah or community into eternity.

Salat (Arabic: "bending at the waist") Public prayer practiced five times each day. One of the Five Pillars.

Sawm (Arabic: "fasting") Fasting from all gratification of appetite, including sexual activity, eating, drinking, etc., especially during Ramadan. One of the Five Pillars.

Shahadah (Arabic: "testimony") The act of confession that there is no God but God and that Muhammad is his prophet. The first of the Five Pillars.

Shari'ah (Arabic: "path to the water hole") The body of Muslim law, drawn from *Sunnah*.

Shi'ism (Arabic: "party, sect") Adherence to the principle that the rightful leadership of the ummah belongs to the descendants of Muhammad through a kind of divine right. Shi'is make up about ten per cent of all Muslims.

Shirk (Arabic: "partner, associate") Associating God with idols, including personal obsessions or false ideals.

Sufi (Arabic: from *tasawwuf*, a coarse woolen garment worn by the poor) The name applied after the first and second centuries to Muslim ascetics and mystics. Later the name of orders or brotherhoods of

Muslims practicing spiritual disciplines under the guidance of a master (*shaikh* or *pir*).

Sujud (Arabic: "bowing") The act of bowing down from the standing position and placing one's forehead on the prayer rug during Salat.

Sunnah (Arabic: "custom, practice") The words and actions of Muhammad considered as normative for the behavior of all Muslims.

Sunnism Adherence to the elective principle of succession embodied in the first four leaders of the ummah after the death of Muhammad and honored by the great majority (ninety per cent) of Muslims, called Sunnis.

Sura (Arabic: "wall") A chapter of the Qur'an.

Takbir (Arabic: "Let him be extolled") The invitation to praise what one has heard or seen as a manifestation of God's will. The reponse is "Allahu akbar" ("God, there is none greater").

Taqwa (Arabic: "attentiveness") Total commitment of body, mind, and heart to the praise of God.

Tauhid (Arabic: "making one") Asserts Islam's monotheism, the fundamental belief that God is One, to which Muslims respond by trying their best to integrate their worship and their lives according to the primary human vocation of praising God.

Ummah (Arabic: "community") The community of those who believe in the revelations coming down to them through Muhammad.

Wali (Arabic: "friend, patron") The Muslim in his or her inner, contemplative, introverted dimension.

Zakat (Arabic: "purification") The purification of wealth by a donation of a fixed percentage of yearly income to the poor. One of the Five Pillars.

Notes

i   John S. Dunne, *The Way of All the Earth* (New York: Macmillan Publishing Co., Inc., 1972), 44.

ii   Ibid., 53.

iii   Fazlur Rahman, *The Major Themes of the Qur'an* (Minneapolis, MN: Biblioteca Islamica, Inc., 1989), 28.

iv   Ibid., 9.

v   Ibid., 127.

vi   Imam Abu Zakariya Yahya bin Sharaf An-Nawawi, ed. *Riyadh-us-Saleheen* [Garden for the Righteous Ones], 4th ed. (New Delhi, India: Kitab Bhavan, 1994), 87.

vii   Michael Sells, ed., *Early Islamic Mysticism: Sufi, Qur'an, Mi'raj, Poetic, and Theoretical Writings* (New York: Paulist Press, 1996), 157.

viii   *Al-kitabul-qaddus* [The Bible]. (*Darul-kitabi al-qaddus fil-sharqil-awsat* [House of the Bible in the Middle East], n.d.). A Protestant edition, since the deuterocanonical books are not included.

ix   Quoted in Karen Armstrong, *Holy War: The Crusades and their Impact on Today's World* (New York: Anchor Books, 2001), 3.

x   Simone Weil, "Concerning the Our Father," in George A. Panichas, ed., *The Simone Weil Reader* (Mt. Kisco, NY: Moyer Bell Limited, 1977), 403.